Living for the End Times

2010

Dr. Delron Shirley

Cover design by Konya Ferrell

This teaching manual is intended for personal study; however, the author encourages all students to also become teachers and to share the truths from this text with others. However, copying the text itself without permission from the author is considered plagiarism which is punishable by law. To obtain permission to quote material from this book, please contact:
Delron Shirley
3210 Cathedral Spires Dr.
Colorado Springs, CO 80904
teachallnations@msn.com
www.teachallnationsmission.com

Table of Contents

Signs of the Times	1
The End Is Near! Or Is It?	1
The Fig Tree Parable	9
Gog and Magog	18
History in the Crosshairs	23
Until the Number is Complete	28
Discerning the Times	32
Discerning the Signs	32
Accurately and Precisely Discerning the Voice of God	39
Three Hindrances	44
A Vision Whose Time Has Not Yet Come	50
God's Will	53
Three Filters	56
Three Responses	61
Lights in a Dark World	66
Responding to the Times	67
Where Can We Look in Times Like These?	69
How Shall We Live, Knowing That the End is Near?	76
He That Hath an Ear	78
Ephesus--Predicament of Passion	80
Smyrna--Presence of Persecution	99
Pergamos--Pitfalls of Permissiveness	113
Thyatira--Problem of Perversion	121
Sardis--Probing Perfection	125
Philadelphia--Purity of Purpose	129
Laodicea--Perplexity of Perception	159
Having Ears to Hear	165
Seeking the Glory of the Nations	168

Signs of the Times

The End Is Near! Or Is It?

As my wife and I were busying ourselves about the kitchen one day, she asked me to check the time. Looking up at the read-out display on our microwave which serves as our kitchen clock when it is not in use, I responded, "It's the end time." Apparently, someone had failed to hit the "clear" button after the last use of the microwave and it was stuck with the message, "END." Is my microwave accurate? Is it really the end time?

When I was growing up, every time we had a cool snap in the middle of the summer or an unseasonably warm day in the middle of the winter my grandmother would say, "It's a sign that the Lord is coming back soon because the Bible says that in the last days you won't be able to tell summer from winter." No matter how many times we tried to tell her that this particular omen wasn't included in the list of signs of the end, we were never able to convince her. Likewise, every time we hear about natural catastrophes such as earthquakes, cyclones, hurricanes, and tsunamis, there are prognosticators who surface to predict that the end is near. Of course, all it takes is a report of the widespread decline in morality, the onslaught of the global AIDS epidemic, or the increase in the crime rate for church people to start panicking over the impending doomsday. Global warming and the failing economy, not to even mention politics (including elections in the US and despots in power around the world) are also great fodder for apocalyptic forecasts. The Doomsday Clock, a symbolic clock face maintained since 1947 by the board of directors of the <u>Bulletin of the Atomic Scientists</u> at the University of Chicago, predicts that the human race is only minutes away from midnight--its catastrophic destruction. Originally, the analogy represented the threat of global nuclear war but now includes climate-change and new developments in the life sciences and nanotechnology that could inflict irrevocable harm. Recently, the clock's hands were set at only five minutes before the "witching hour" due to the build up of nuclear weapons, terrorism, and climate change. The scientific world seems to have taken literally over the job of Chicken Little, running around telling us that the sky is falling by predicting that we are on a collision course with asteroids that will destroy our present civilization the same way that they claim the dinosaurs were eradicated some sixty-five billion years ago. If it isn't a scientist or politician threatening us with global warming, it is an evangelist warning us of the last days--but we are getting the same message from every side: we are headed for TETWAWKI, the end of the world as we know it.

  Forty percent of all Americans and forty-five percent of Christians believe that there will be a final battle between Jesus Christ and the Antichrist at Armageddon. A recent poll showed that seventy-one percent of evangelical Protestants, twenty-eight percent of non-evangelicals, and eighteen percent of Catholics believe that the scenario will take place. About half of those who share the belief said that they think that the Antichrist is living today, and forty-five percent said Jesus Christ will return before they die. Most who believe in the Second Coming of Christ say that the world is experiencing the "end times." Many believe that current events signify that the end is near: eighty-three percent cited the spate of natural disasters, sixty-six percent noted diseases such as AIDS and the Ebola virus, and sixty-two percent said outbreaks of violence are signs of the end.

Of course, we can look back through history and see that we are not unique in our doomsday beliefs. I remember so well back in 1988 when Jim Willis' Armageddon Now: the End of the World A to Z swept so many in the Christian community into apocalyptic frenzy with eight-eight reasons why Jesus was to return that year. You can't imagine my embarrassment as the associate pastor every time I would see a certain car parked in our church parking lot--it was painted from bumper to bumper with prophecies of the imminent end of the world! I've often wondered what the gentleman did with his car on January 1, 1989. Many Christians felt that AD 1000 was the end of the Millennium and tried to force non-believers into conversion before "the end" came. William Miller, the father of the modern Adventist movement, predicted the end between March 21, 1843, and March 21, 1844. He later recalculated the date to be October 22, 1844, which became known as "the Great Disappointment" because many of his followers sold all they had in order to be ready for the end--which simply didn't happen. The 1910 appearance of Halley's Comet prompted many apocalyptic fears, including the publication of a post card in Germany which read, "End of the World on May 18." Albert Porta, a well respected meteorologist, predicted the end of the world on December 17, 1919, due to the conjunction of six planets which he said would cause a magnetic current that would pierce the sun causing great explosions of flaming gases that would engulf the earth. In 1936, Edger Cayce predicted that the world would end through a major reconfiguration of the continents, the reappearance of the lost continent of Atlantis near the Bahamas, the disappearance of California and Japan, and violent volcanic eruptions worldwide. When his prediction failed, he recalculated the date for 1998, apparently giving himself the benefit of not having to face another missed calculation--that is assuming that he would not live past 120 years old! In 1967, aliens in UFOs told George Van Tassel that the southeastern portion of the US would be destroyed by a nuclear attack. Essentially the entire world approached Y2K with a sense of dread as they feared that massive computer failures would send the world into a virtual TETWAWKI with planes hurling helter-skelter through the skies as the air traffic controls blacked out, patients dying agonizing deaths as their life-support systems shut down, criminals escaping even maximum-security penitentiaries as the surveillance systems melted down, and the skylines of cities worldwide disappearing as the electric grids collapsed. The fortieth anniversary of the Six Day War (2007) was highlighted by many evangelical leaders including Pat Robertson. The Mayan calendar of the Central American Indians abruptly ends on the winter solstice of December 21, 2012 (their year 5,126) when the sun will be aligned with the center of the Milky Way for the first time in 26,000 years, paralleling the Hopi Indian belief that a blue star will appear in 2012 signaling the return of Saquasohuh who will usher in a new age. Jean Dixon, the psychic who predicted the assassination of President John F. Kennedy, gave us eight more years by predicting that Armageddon will happen in 2020. St. Malachy, who was born in 1094, predicted that there would be one hundred twelve more popes from his time. Since the present pontiff is number one hundred eleven, we can see that his prediction also puts us at the brink of TETWAWKI.

    But do any of these prophecies of the end of the world as we know it have any real significance? Of all the dates suggested above, only four of them have any real relationship to biblical chronology: AD 1000, 1988, 2000, and 2007. The AD 1000 date was based on the idea that the Millennium, the thousand year rule of Christ predicted in Revelation 20:6, had begun with Jesus' birth. The fault with this calculation is that the Millennium is to begin <u>after</u> TETWAWKI, not as its initiation.

The 2000 date which just coincidentally paralleled the scientific Y2K calculation was based on the concept that God created the universe in six days and then rested on the seventh. Those who say the year 2000 as the date for TETWAWKI paralleled His creative work with His redemptive work and said that if He created the world in six days, He would also complete His redemptive work in six days. Since II Peter 3:8 equates one day as a thousand years, they then calculate that it would take six thousand years of human history to do so. By counting the genealogies of the Bible, they calculate that the creation of Adam occurred about 4000 BC, naming AD 2000 the six thousandth year. Since God rested on the seventh day and the thousand years following human history on earth is to be the Millennium, another period of divine rest, the analogy seemed quite proper in many people's minds.

The other two of the more modern dates are both calculations based on Luke chapter twenty-one verses twenty-four and thirty-two. "And they shall fall by the edge of the sword, and shall be led away captive into all nations: and Jerusalem shall be trodden down of the Gentiles, until the times of the Gentiles be fulfilled...Verily I say unto you, This generation shall not pass away, till all be fulfilled." In this prophetic discourse, Jesus gave a couple predictions which can be linked together as a historical starting point and a duration for the countdown. The first starting date is based on the declaration of the independent state of Israel on May 15, 1948. Since Israel had been under gentile domination since the Romans destroyed Jerusalem in AD 70, the re-establishment of the Jewish state was seen as the fulfillment of Jesus' prediction that the Holy City would come out from under the foot of foreigners. However, there was one major flaw in this calculation. The United Nations' decision which established the nation of Israel actually carved the Holy Land and the city of Jerusalem into somewhat of a jigsaw puzzle, giving parts to Israel and parts to the Palestinians. Since the actual ancient city of Jerusalem was under Jordanian jurisdiction, it would be impossible to see this as the fulfillment of Jesus' prophecy. One thing I've noticed about Jesus is that He tends to say what He means and mean what He says; therefore, if He said that the Holy City would no longer be trodden under the feet of the gentiles, I'm sure that He would not settle for some territory in the general vicinity! The second start date was based on the capture of the ancient city of Jerusalem during the Six Day War of 1967. On June 10, 1967, the Israeli army concluded their blitz against their Arab neighbors and walked away in possession of the city of Jerusalem, the actual soil that Jesus had mentioned in His prophecy! For the first time since the Roman conquest of the city, Jews could freely and safely walk the streets of their holy city and call it their own! However, the Temple Mount is still under control of Muslims; therefore, at least one part of the Holy City is still trodden by gentile feet. So maybe 1967 is not our actual start date either.

Verse thirty-two gives us the duration of the countdown period from the starting point to the culmination as one generation. According to many biblical and prophecy scholars, a generation can be considered a forty-year period. However, a generation may not necessarily be forty years; perhaps it could be a full lifespan of seventy or eighty years. (Psalm 90:10) Perhaps the reference could even suggest that a person who is born on the start date would see the fulfillment on the last day of his life, making a generation as long as a hundred years. Obviously, the world did not end either in 1988 or 2007, so one or all of the factors mentioned above must have been in play. Let's see if there are further clues that we can watch for.

When they look at Jesus' predictions of TETWAWKI, most preachers and teachers reference Matthew chapter twenty-four and its parallels in Mark chapter thirteen and Luke chapter twenty-one, wanting to focus in on some of the sensational indicators that Jesus mentioned: the advent of false christs, wars, rumors of wars, nations rising against nations, kingdoms rising against kingdoms, famines, pestilences, and earthquakes. However, Jesus plainly told us that these are only the beginnings of sorrows (Matthew 24:8) and that they are not the final indicators of the end (verse 6). He then goes on to give us some specific pointers to watch for: Christians will be delivered up to be afflicted and killed in every nation (verse 9), many will be offended and will betray and hate one another (verse 10), false prophets will arise (verse 11), the love of many shall wax cold (verse 12), and the gospel of the kingdom will be preached in all the world (verse 14). It is then that He declares that the end will come. Jesus also said that the condition among the inhabitants of the planet at the time of his return would be identical to those at the times of Noah and Lot. (Luke 17:26-30) The Apostle Paul added a few indicators when he analyzed the conditions that would exist in the last days: men will be lovers of themselves, covetous, boasters, proud, blasphemers, disobedient to parents, unthankful, unholy, without natural affection, trucebreakers, false accusers, incontinent, fierce, despisers of those that are good, traitors, heady, high-minded, lovers of pleasures more than lovers of God, followers of a form of religion that denies His power. (II Timothy 3:5) The Apostle Peter added that the end time would be characterized by scoffers walking after their own lusts. (II Peter 3:3)

Much of the prophetic teaching of today's church centers around explanations of ten toes, four horses, seventy years, seven vials, two witnesses, one hundred forty-four thousand evangelists, the mark of the six hundred sixty-six, and the thousand-year reign. Yet we have often overlooked the one thing in prophecy that so personally affects us--the two who have become one, our homes. Jesus Christ prophesied divorce and remarriage, pornography, and homosexuality (Matthew 24:37-38, Luke 17:28). Paul of Tarsus prophesied run-away kids, rebellious children, teen pregnancies, abortion, euthanasia, child abuse, homosexuality, divorce, and unwed couples (II Timothy 3:2-3, I Timothy 4:3). The Old Testament prophet Zephaniah (verse 1:18) and the New Testament apostle James (verse 5:3) predicted economic collapse in the end times. Daniel prophesied a dramatic increase in travel and education. (verse 12:4) Both the Old and New Testaments (Joel 2:28-29, Acts 2:17-18) add one other indicator of the last days, a universal outpouring of the Holy Spirit.

We could spend pages on the moral condition of the human race as predicted by Jesus and Paul. But regardless of all that could be said concerning immorality and corruption in the world today, it would be difficult to use those statistics as to pinpoint our present generation as the terminal generation for life as we presently know it on Planet Earth. However, these conditions are too subjective to use as a definite sign of end. Writers of almost every generation have described their generation in apocalyptic terms. In fact, I have read some publications from previous centuries which were powerfully convincing that the human condition fit the biblical description of the end time; however, the world did not end then--and we can't be sure that the lifestyles of today are the final fulfillment of prophesy. Therefore, let's focus our attention on a couple issues that might be a bit more quantifiable. But first, I'd like to draw your attention to the context of the whole discussion that the disciples had with Jesus when He told them about TETWAWKI.

The Fig Tree Parable

With the sound of the exuberant crowd still echoing in his ears, Jesus ducked away from the throngs to look around the temple. It would almost seem out-of-place for the Palm Sunday triumphant entry to be so anti-climatically punctuated--that is unless we read and understand the passages which follow Mark 11:11. Immediately after this glorious entry into Jerusalem where He was being boisterously proclaimed as the promised Son of David and the Messiah, Jesus left the celebrant followers behind and took time to investigate the temple and the activities going on inside it. By doing so, he set the pattern for his activities and teachings of the next few days.

On that very next morning, He stopped on the top of the Mount of Olives to check out a fig tree and find that it was bearing many leaves but no fruit. His response was that the tree was to be cursed and that no man would ever eat fruit of it again. After this seemingly vindictive interlude, Jesus continued his journey into Jerusalem. There, he purged the temple of the money changers and sacrifice sellers. It was also there that the scribes and chief priests plotted together to kill the carpenter-prophet-messiah. The following morning, Jesus and His followers passed by the fig tree again and Peter discovered that now--only twenty-four hours after Jesus' command--the tree was dead and withered from its roots. Jesus responded that not only would fig trees wither but that a whole mountain would be cast into the sea. Those who stood with Jesus as the early morning sun rays beamed across the peak of the Mount of Olives and turned the white stones of Jerusalem and the gleaming marble of the temple to the effervescent hues that gave it the name "Jerusalem of Gold," could think of only one mountain when the teacher's words "this mountain" touched their ears. To them, standing in the spot that is even today the most popular vantage point and the most photographed view of Jerusalem, the only mountain on their minds was the stunning Temple Mount which lay in all its panoramic splendor before them. They may not have taken immediate notice of it, but it wouldn't be too long until they understood that their beloved Jerusalem and Israel would face the same destiny as that withered fig tree.

    That evening, as Jesus and His little band of followers returned to the brow of the Mount of Olives, they paused for a moment to look back at the city of Jerusalem. At that moment, the disciples possibly had no recollection of the fact that earlier that same day Jesus had told them that the mountain of Judaism would face the same demise as the withered fig tree. On top of the mount, they paused to point out the beauty of the scene before them. Jesus jolted them back to the reality of the day by saying that the city was ripe for such utter destruction that not one stone would be left on top of another one. He went on to prophesy the Roman invasion of AD 70 and the subsequent scattering of the Jews among all the nations of the world. The mountain of Judaism was to be cast into the sea of the nations (a prophetic symbol explained in Revelation 17:15).

After a fairly lengthy discussion of the horrors of the future, Jesus added, "Now learn a parable of the fig tree." Certainly, each and every disciple's mind flashed to the fig tree which they had seen wither that morning. Jesus did not say "learn a parable from a fig tree"; He specifically said "the fig tree." Here, just a matter of paces away from the tree which had so dramatically perished only hours before, they couldn't help but realize that the up-coming parable was going to be based on the fruitless tree which had been cursed. Jesus, undoubtedly, shocked them with His next line, "When her branch is yet tender, and she putteth forth leaves..." The withered tree--the one dried up from the very roots--would someday have tender branches again and begin to put out new leaves! Even though Jerusalem was facing utter destruction and Israel was facing a world-wide deportation, God promised that she would live again!

For just short of nineteen centuries, the Jewish people were outcasts from the land of Israel. The real estate which had been deeded to Abraham was trampled under the feet of the Byzantine Empire, the Islamic Arab insurgents, the Catholic Crusades, Saladin and his Muslim successors, the Ottoman

Turks, and the British Mandate administrators. The land lay in a virtual state of mourning that its rightful owners were in exile. No ruling power was able to bring back the glory of Israel's past. The majesty of Solomon's day was gone forever. The glory of David had faded. The land that once flowed with milk and honey became a waste land and--as the prophet of the old would say--"a habitation of dragons." (Isaiah 34:13) Under the Turkish rule, a heavy tax was placed on each tree standing on any piece of property. The result was a denuding of the land that led to erosion and even a climatic change to a more arid and hotter environment. We can readily see the withered fig tree image in the description left us by the great American author Mark Twain when he made his 1869 pilgrimage:

> Of all the lands there are for dismal scenery, I think Palestine must be the prince. The hills are barren, they are dull of color, they are unpicturesque in shape. The valleys are unsightly deserts fringed with a feeble vegetation that has an expression about it of being sorrowful and despondent. The Dead Sea and the Sea of Galilee sleep in the midst of a vast stretch of hill and plain wherein the eye rests upon no pleasant tint, no striking object, no soft picture dreaming in a purple haze or mottled with the shadows of the clouds. Every outline is harsh, every feature is distinct, there is no perspective--distance works no enchantment here. It is a hopeless, dreary, heartbroken land...Palestine sits in sackcloth and ashes. Over it

broods the spell of a curse that has withered its fields and fettered its energies. Palestine is desolate and unlovely. And why should it be otherwise? Can the curse of the Deity beautify a land?

To fully understand the significance of Jesus' parable about the fig tree, we should parallel the time table of the budding of the fig tree which represents the rebirth of the nation of Israel with the budding of "all the trees" (Luke 21:19) which represent the fulfillment of other prophecies of the end of time. As we have already indicated, two of these prophecies include Jesus' statement in Matthew 24:14, "And this gospel of the kingdom shall be preached in all the world for a witness unto all nations, and then shall the end come," and the Apostle Peter's prophecy in Acts 2:17, "It shall come to pass in the last days, saith God, I will pour out of my spirit upon all flesh." From these two passages, we can see that the end of time is to be characterized by world-wide evangelism and a supernatural visitation of the Holy Spirit. Interestingly enough, each time a new leaf has begun to bud in Israel, a new wave of evangelism and spiritual activity has occurred.

In 1897, Theodor Herzl hosted the first Zionist Congress which led to the desire to re-establish a Jewish homeland. That same time period witnessed a great shift in technology and spiritual movement. Certain new inventions had to be brought into being in order for all the nations of the earth to be reached with the gospel. One necessary invention was the airplane. For the whole world to come into the grasp of evangelists, a remarkably faster form of transportation had to be birthed--and it was on the sandy hills of Kitty Hawk, NC, when Orville and Wilbur Wright made their first forty-yard flight in 1903. Another necessary innovation was the mass communication tool of radio. For one message to reach the whole world, a vehicle for spreading the message had to be birthed--and it was when Guglielmo Marconi sent the first radio message in 1895 and R. A. Fessenden sent the first voice broadcast in the year 1900. These two inventions moved the church into a whole new mode of evangelism. It was also at the turn of the century that a whole new wave of the supernatural began to sweep across the globe. This spiritual explosion detonated at the Azusa Street Mission in Los Angeles in 1906 and soon echoed around the world. Just like the age-old dream for a homeland in the heart of the disposed Jew was now coming to pass and the unthinkable notions of defying gravity and space were suddenly coming into human grasp, the church was suddenly heir to an almost forgotten promise of the floods of the latter rain of the Holy Spirit in the time of harvest.

As we follow the development of the buds on Israel's fig tree, we can note several important stages. At each point that the fig tree's leaves unrolled, we can see that there was also an intensification of the movement of the Holy Spirit and a development in world evangelism. On May 15, 1948, Israel was declared an independent nation. In the arena of world evangelism, God was also doing supernatural things. This was the beginning of the great healing revival--the second wave of the Holy Spirit's outpouring. It was in that year that Oral Roberts incorporated his non-taxable religious corporation. William Branham, T.L. Osborne, and Billy Graham also got their starts in evangelism at this time. In the area of communications and travel, television and commercial air travel were just coming into their own. It was also in 1948 that the transistor was invented, opening the way for radios and televisions to become household items around the world.

In July of 1956, Egypt seized the Suez Canal from its British and French owners. This aggression culminated in an Israeli attack through the Sinai Desert. In the church, 1956 was a year of marked attacks against the move of God. In both the US and Britain, the national medical associations took official stances against divine healing, and some healing evangelists were actually taken to court on the grounds of practicing medicine without a license.

In 1967, after several threatening actions by the surrounding Arab states, Israel decided to strike before being struck. On June 5, Israeli planes simultaneously attacked bases in Egypt, Jordan, and Syria. In the ensuing Six Day War, Israel took the Gaza Strip, the Sinai Peninsula, the West Bank, the Old City of Jerusalem, and the Golan Heights. In the church, an unprecedented charismatic move of God swept into the Catholic Church.

On Yom Kippur in 1973, when the entire Israeli army was in fasting and no national broadcast service was operating, Egypt and Syria attacked Israel, but found Israel to be unsinkable even at her most unprepared moments. Just at this period of history, the Word and Faith movement was beginning to emerge. This was a new breed of men and women of God who dared to believe the promises of God's Word and act in faith to see them fulfilled. Fearlessly they went after and obtained whatever the Lord offered them. These were men who knew how to believe God for millions of dollars in order to reach millions of lost souls.

Lester Sumrall, just one example, took hold of the technology of the twentieth century and led the

Christian world into mass evangelism by radio and television. By the time of his death in 1996, he operated a whole network of nearly a dozen television stations, a local FM radio station, twenty-four-hour-a-day satellite broadcasting, and five shortwave stations covering the entire globe with the full gospel evangelical message! He also took hold of the modern transportation system and became the first non-governmental operation to own a military-type C-130 plane for transporting food, medical supplies, gospel literature, and other relief materials to the needy nations of the world.

    Concerning the universal outpouring of the Holy Spirit, Vinson Synan, Regent University professor and historian of the Pentecostal movement, estimates that more than one forth of the world's Christians are Pentecostal or charismatic. He said that there are almost two billion people who profess the Christian faith, and that more than half a billion of them are charismatic or Pentecostal. He sites South Korea as an example of how the faith has impacted a whole nation. In 1900, the country was considered one of the most resistant mission fields in the world. Today, thirty percent of the population is Christian, making Christianity the largest faith group in the nation. About sixty percent of Korean Christians are Pentecostal.

    Concerning Jesus' promise in Matthew 24:14 that the gospel of the kingdom will be preached to every ethnic group before the Lord's return, John Elliott, director of World Outreach, says that there is a real possibility that every unreached people group will have the gospel within twenty to thirty years! Even though over six thousand of the world's approximately sixteen thousand ethnic groups are still considered unreached and over two and a half billion of the world's almost seven billion citizens are members of these unreached groups, and only twenty-four hundred of the planet's almost seven thousand currently spoken languages have some or all of the Bible, the advancements in technology and the anointing of the Spirit upon today's ministries is causing an explosive rate of advancement like never before known. For example, in the early 1990s, missiologists estimated there were fourteen thousand language groups without access to a viable church. Elliott reported that within just a little over a decade that number was reduced to about six thousand.

Although we cannot find any unquestionably specific reference to the United States in biblical prophecy, I'd like to take just a minute to consider the possibility that she may be seen as somehow included among the "other trees" which are to bud in the last days. April 29, 2007, marked the four hundredth anniversary of the first English-speaking prayer meeting on American soil. Having left their homes in England around Christmas of 1606, the colonists had originally tried to come ashore on the beaches of Virginia as soon as they reached land after their grueling journey across the Atlantic. However, an attack by the Chesapeake Indians left them injured and scurrying back aboard. Upon returning to the ship, the exploration party's young Anglican chaplain, Robert Hunt, suggested that the company regroup to pray for three days. Only after purifying their hearts and spirits did they make a second attempt as Chaplain Hunt led them ashore on what is now known as Cape Henry. Upon reaching the beachhead, the settlers held a prayer service, planted a cross on the sand dunes, dedicated the new land to God's purposes, and declared that the Gospel would be carried to the entire world from those shores. And God did answer that prayer in that the United States of America, with only nineteen percent of the world's Protestants and twenty-one percent of the world's evangelicals, would eventually rise to the preeminent position of missions leadership by producing seventy percent of the present missions force and eighty percent of missions funding. It seems to me that there might be something prophetic about this four hundredth anniversary of that historic prayer meeting in which it was proclaimed that the gospel would go out to the ends of the earth from the shores of this new land. There was four hundred years of silence from the last word of the terminal prophet in the Old Testament until the birth of Jesus in Bethlehem--four hundred years of incubation anticipating the manifestation of God's incarnate son. There was also four hundred years between the time when Joseph passed from the scene of action in Egypt and the rise of Moses as the deliverer of the Israelites--four hundred years of slavery awaiting a great deliverance. Is it possible that these most recent four centuries have been only the preparation for the last great missionary thrust that will bring the gospel of the kingdom to every nation under heaven? Is it time for another unprecedented move of the Holy Spirit? Is it time for another bud to burst forth from the withered fig tree?

Gog and Magog
It happens that we know a bit of pre-written history concerning Israel's future. Beginning in chapter thirty-six of his prophetic book, Ezekiel prophesied the return of the Jews to their homeland and the rebirth of their nation--the budding of the fig leaves, if you please. In chapter thirty-eight, he described a dramatic conflict

in a play-by-play action report. This scenario has to do with the nation of Russia and her attempt against Israel. According to the prophetic word, Gog of the land of Magog--the chief prince of Mesheck and Tubal--will align himself with Persia, Ethiopia, Libya, Gomor, Togarrmah, and many other people to attack a land brought back from the sword. Bible scholars concur that this refers to Russia in alliance with Iran, Iraq, Moslem Africa, and Germany. An interesting term is used in verse four where God says, "I will put hooks in your jaws." Although I don't consider myself a great angler, I do know one thing from the few fish I have managed to get on a line: the hook is a means of bringing an unwilling subject to an undesired location! God is declaring here that He will pull Russia against her will into a conflict in Israel. Is there anything happening in the world today that could possibly become a hook which could draw Russia into aggressive attack against Israel? Perhaps it can be seen in Russia's connection with Iran. In the past few years, Russia--the world's leading arms dealer--has increased its military shipments to Iran. In fact, the value of the arms transfer agreements between Iran and Russia ballooned from $300 million between 1998 and 2001 to $1.7 billion between 2002 and 2005. It is suspected that many of these weapons eventually wound up the hands of radical groups such as the Hezbollah and the Hamas. Since 1992, Russia has sold Iran hundreds of major weapons systems, including tanks, air-to-air missiles, and combat aircraft. They have also agreed to sell Iran a surface-to-air missile defense system along with air-defense missile systems to defend its soon-to-be-completed Russian-built nuclear reactor. There are also plans to upgrade Tehran's military with Russian anti-aircraft missiles which can intercept enemy aircraft from ninety to one hundred eighty miles away. Iran is also building up its naval presence with Russian-made high-speed torpedoes capable of destroying large warships or submarines. These weapons are going to a nation whose leaders believe that it is their divine destiny to usher in the return of the Islamic messiah by destroying Israel (the Small Satan) and the United States (the Great Satan). Their feverish attempts to build, buy, or steal nuclear weapons in their attempt to trigger the End of Days continue to push them deeper and deeper into an alliance with Russia. All the while, Israel is making no secret of her concern over Iran's development of nuclear weaponry. Many of Israel's leaders feel that the international community is looking to them--and even expecting them--to launch a strike against Iran to stop their progress toward nuclear armament. Efraim Inbar of the Begin-Sadat Center for Strategic Studies at Tel Aviv's Bar-han University analyzed the present situation, "They will be very happy if we do their dirty work for them. The world is moving into 'What can we do about it?' mode. There is a strong instinct here to do it on our own." To many in Israel, the situation is reminiscent of 1981 when the Jewish state acted on its own in bombing the Osirak reactor in Iraq and 2007 when it launched a unilateral strike on a suspected nuclear site in Syria. Many in Israel see a narrow window in which to act. "Time is running very, very short right now," said Ephraim Asculai, a longtime veteran of the Israeli Atomic Energy Commission. If Israel does act, Russia will no doubt be pulled as if with a hook in her jaw into retaliation.

Ezekiel gives a dramatic description of the decimation of the Russian horde which will result from their attack.

And it shall come to pass at the same time when Gog shall come against the land of Israel, saith the Lord God, that my fury shall come up in my face. For in my jealousy and in the fire of my wrath have I spoken, Surely in that day there shall be a great shaking in the land of Israel; So that the fishes of the sea, and the fowls of the heaven, and the beasts of the field, and all creeping things that are upon the face of the earth, shall shake at my presence, and the mountains shall be thrown down, and the steep places shall fall, and every wall shall fall to the ground. And I will call for a sword against him throughout all my mountains, saith the Lord God: every man's sword shall be against his brother. And I will plead against him with pestilence and with blood; and I will rain upon him, and upon his bands, and upon the many people that are with him, and overflowing rain, and great hailstones, fire, and brimstone. Thus will I magnify myself, and sanctify myself; and I will be known in the eyes of many nations, and they shall know that I am the Lord. Therefore, thou son of man, prophesy against Gog, and say, Thus saith the Lord God; Behold, I am against thee, O Gog, the chief prince of Mesheck and Tubal: And I will turn thee back, and leave but the sixth part of thee, and will cause thee to come up from the north parts, and will bring thee upon the mountains of Israel: And I will smite thy bow out of thy left hand, and will cause thine arrows to fall out of thy right hand. Thou shalt fall upon the mountains of Israel, thou, and all thy bands, and the people that is with thee: I will give thee unto the ravenous birds of every sort, and to the beasts of the field to be devoured. Thou shalt fall upon the open field: for I have spoken it, saith the Lord God. And I will send a fire on Magog and among them that dwell carelessly in the isles: and they shall know that I am the Lord. So will I make my holy name known in the midst of my people Israel; and I will not let them pollute my holy name any more: and the heathen shall know that I am the Lord, the Holy One of Israel. Behold, it is come, and it is done, saith the Lord God; this is the day whereof I have spoken. And they that dwell in the cities of Israel shall go forth, and shall set on fire and burn the weapons, both the shields and the bucklers, the bows and the arrows, and the handstaves, and the spears, and they shall burn them with fire seven years: So that they shall take no wood out of the field, neither cut down any out of the forests; for they shall burn the weapons with fire: and they shall spoil those that spoiled them, saith the Lord God. And it shall come to pass in that day, that I will give unto Gog a place there of graves in Israel, the valley of the passengers on the east of the sea: and it shall stop the noses of the passengers: and there shall they bury Gog and all his multitude: and they shall call it The valley of Hamon-gog. And seven months shall the house of Israel be burying of them, that they may cleanse the land. (Ezekiel 38:18-39:12)

Perhaps this destruction of the invasion forces will be the next event--possibly the final one--that will allow Israel to extend her boundaries to the prophesied limits of the Euphrates River and set in motion the prophecies concerning rise to power of the Antichrist and his eventual move against the covenant land and people.

If this bud does begin to unfold, we can also expect a dramatic new wave of world evangelism and a new outpouring of the Holy Spirit. And, in deed, the time is ripe for both.

History in the Crosshairs

Galatians 4:4 says that God sent forth His son into the world in the fullness of the time. If we stop to think about it, we will realize that the time when Jesus came to sojourn among us earthlings was a unique "crosshairs moment" in the history of the human race.

In the succession of empires, the Romans had recently conquered the Greeks and established Pax Roma (the Roman peace) throughout the then-known world. Because of their world-wide domination and the force with which the Romans ruled the subjugated nations, history saw its first universal open-door policy allowing citizens of any area to freely travel to any other region over which the Roman flag fluttered. The ever-present Roman militia guarded the highways and ports, ensuring a previously unknown security for travelers. Not only was travel safer than at any point previously, it was also more convenient and practical than at any point previous. In order to guarantee quick movement of their troops to any corner of their empire, the Romans had engineered a remarkably advanced highway system linking even the most far-flung regions. When two millennia later we use the expression, "All roads lead to Rome," we are still attesting to the existence of the intricate highway system that marked the days of the Roman Empire. These roadways were nothing less than engineering marvels of their day. In fact, I have personally driven for miles on their ancient road beds and ridden across their bridges that have stood for over two thousand years and today carry the full load of modern automobile, trucks, and busses. But what does the Roman highway system have to do with the birth of the Messiah? Everything--because He came to proclaim the acceptable year of the Lord (Luke 4:19) and that message could not travel to the ends of the earth without a good highway system and safe passage for the messengers who were to carry it--a reality under the Roman rule which would have been nothing more than a pipe dream in any previous generation.

    Not only did God send His Son into the world when transportation was uniquely possible, He also sent His Son at a remarkably specific moment when the entire world understood one amazingly precise language. When Alexander the Great died in his drunken stupor lamenting that at age thirty-three there were no more worlds for him to conquer, he left behind an empire sweeping around the Mediterranean and sprawling as far as India--an empire which would soon be unified by the Greek language and philosophy. The Hellenizers who would march in behind him had no doubt that the Greek culture was immeasurably superior to any civilization under their domination. With unflagging zeal and devotion, they set about the task of converting each conquered people to their language and philosophy. Before long, one universal language dominated in education, legal matters, and literature. Again we may ask ourselves what this has to do with the coming of Christ. And again we must answer "Everything"--because Jesus came into the world as the Word of God (John 1:1) and that word needed to be understood accurately and correctly. No other language has ever graced human lips with as precise a vocabulary and syntax with which to covey its message. With more verb forms and more explicit definitions than any other language, Greek was the idea vehicle to covey the greatest story ever told. Not only was the language extraordinarily precise, it was universal. Until the exact moment in which Christ entered the scene, there had not been another point in history since the Tower of Babel when there was the possibility of presenting the message in one language and expecting that it would be able to be understood no matter how many miles it would cross. Prior to the spread of the Greek language, the message would likely not be understood on the next corner, much less another continent.

    Not only was the world politically, linguistically, and physically prepared for God's miraculous message, it was spiritually pregnant in anticipation of a divine invasion. All of the major world religions of the time were in a state of flux, essentially redefining themselves. Although Hinduism had existed for a thousand years, it was going through its greatest period of crystallization at precisely the point in which Jesus came. Siddhartha Gautama had experienced his enlightenment some five hundred prior, but Buddhism as a codified religion was just emerging at the time that the Christmas star appeared in the eastern sky. Of course, Judaism is the religion of the Old Testament, or is it? Listen to the rabbis and read the scholarly books of the faith and you will find that the real foundation upon which their beliefs are based is the Talmud, a collection of the sayings of their rabbis--a collection which was only brought together and preserved in writing at the time that the Christian faith was being birthed. Not only were these living faiths in their adolescent stages, reaching their spiritual puberty; but two other major religions were passing from adulthood to old age and were ready to die. The mythology of the Greek and Roman religions had stood as explanations of nature and the meaning of life for centuries; yet just as BC gave way to AD, the masses began to see these stories for what they really were--nothing more than fables and the imagery of old men's imaginations. Again, we ask what does this have to do with the coming of the Messiah. And again we answer, "Everything"--because Jesus came into the world to save men from their sins (Matthew 1:21), something that men would not accept as long as they felt secure in their own religions.

It was into a world where every major element had come to a focal point that Jesus came in His first advent. And it will be into a world that is just as much in the crosshairs that He will come in His second advent. That world will be one in which men can freely travel from one end of the globe to the other in order to communicate the end-time message of the gospel--a world like the one we live in today. Just two centuries ago when William Carey left the shores of Brittan as the first modern Protestant missionary, he faced five months at sea before he would set foot on Indian soil. Today, we can reach any place on the face of the earth, preach the gospel, set up a church, and head back home in less time than Carey had to contend with seasickness. The world to which Jesus will appear in His Second Coming will be a world which will be able to hear the message in one universal media--a world like the one we live in today. When Wycliffe USA, a Bible translating organization, received an anonymous gift of $50 million in late 2008, they announced that the funding would allow them to use cutting-edge translation techniques to accelerate the pace of language development and Bible translation for the world's remaining language groups. The previous estimate that it would take between a hundred and one hundred fifty years to complete the task was cut overnight to a mere seventeen years! When Jesus returns, He will come back to a world whose religions have failed them--a world like the one in which we live today. According to researcher George Barna, American churchgoers don't feel they are communicating with God. Only about seventy-five million of the three hundred million people who live in America attend church every Sunday--and most of them don't believe that attending church has helped them experience God's presence. Less than a third of those who go to church feel they are interacting with God during service and an additional third said they have never experienced God's presence. The world is again in the crosshairs, ready for the appearance of the Messiah.

Until the Number is Complete
There is one other indicator that we must not overlook, Jesus' statement that Christians were to be hated and killed in all nations--a prophecy that He re-emphasized as part of His last instructions to His disciples.

> These things have I spoken unto you, that ye should not be offended. They shall put you out of the synagogues: yea, the time cometh, that whosoever killeth you will think that he doeth God service. And these things will they do unto you, because they have not known the Father, nor me. If the world hate you, ye know that it hated me before it hated you. If ye were of the world, the world would love his own: but because ye are not of the world, but I have chosen you out of the world, therefore the world hateth you. Remember the word that I said unto you, The servant is not greater than his lord. If they have persecuted me, they will also persecute you; if they have kept my saying, they will keep yours also. But all these things will they do unto you for my name's sake, because they know not him that sent me. (John 15:1-3, 18-21)

As I read these words from our Master, I am convinced that Jesus is talking about a universal persecution which will engulf the church world-wide.

The church has always known persecution; remember the Christians versus the lions. I once saw a cartoon depicting a modern-day man watching a television program about the early Christians being fed to the lions in the Roman amphitheater. The caption read, "Christianity didn't used to be a spectator sport." A follow-up line added, "It still isn't." The truth is that today the Christian faith is experiencing more widespread attacks than at any other time in history. More Christians were slaughtered in the past century than the total causalities in World War I, World War II, the Vietnam War, and the Korean War combined! Yet, most of us have no concept that over two hundred million of our Christian brothers and sisters around the world live under severe conditions of oppression and persecution. Most of us have no realization what it means that these believers live under a constant threat of imprisonment, torture, slavery, and even death. Most of us are totally foreign to the fact that blood is being spilled every day on behalf of the gospel which we so nonchalantly take as a given in our lives. Thousands of martyrs are being slaughtered in countries which have Moslem, Buddhist, Hindu, or other anti-Christian controlled governments. Religious fanaticism is causing problems for Christians in many parts of the world. "Destroy all Christian churches today!" scream typical headlines In prominent Hindu newspapers. Some papers have openly called for a campaign of genocide against non-Hindus who refuse to deny Jesus Christ and convert to Hinduism. Death threats are common both in print and on the field. The Buddhist controlled governments of some Asian countries have been working on exterminating entire tribes of hundreds of thousands of people simply because they are predominately Christians. Modern helicopter gun ships and armies have been used in some areas to exterminate entire population regions of

Christians.

Several years ago, a little insert encouraging us to pray for the persecuted church was enclosed in our church bulletin. One startling sentence was emblazoned into my heart as I took the few minutes necessary to read the flier: "By the time you finish reading this page, another brother or sister will have given his or her life for the faith." One believer is martyred every three and a half minutes. That means that while most churches are making their announcements, one of our brothers has been announced at the Pearly Gates as a new arrival through martyrdom; while we sing one worship song, one of our sisters has performed the ultimate act of worship; in the time it takes most churches to receive the offering, two of our brothers or sisters have made the most acceptable offering possible.

When we realize the suffering that our brothers and sisters are enduring, the Holy Spirit will begin to motivate us to pray as He did Bob Pierce, the founder of World Vision, "Oh Lord, break my heart with the things that break yours!" Jesus Himself interceded for Peter when He realized that the disciple was headed into a trying ordeal.

> And the Lord said, Simon, Simon, behold, Satan hath desired to have you, that he may sift you as wheat: But I have prayed for thee, that thy faith fail not: and when thou art converted, strengthen thy brethren. (Luke 22:31-32)

As tragic as it is that such atrocities actually occur, it is equally tragic that we find it almost impossible to relate to the fact that they are actually occurring. To all but a few of us, such horrors are always "over there some where in another part of the world." According to Mathew 24:9, there is coming a day when this kind of hatred and persecution will be universal. According to Jesus, it will happen in every nation--and I somehow believe that He was predicting something more severe than the banning of prayer in schools, the dropping of "under God" from the Pledge of Allegiance, the removal of the Ten Commandments from public buildings, and the forbidding of Nativity scenes on courthouse lawns. If we are really anticipating that these are the end days, we must brace ourselves to live out our faith in the face of every kind of abuse and to be ready to literally walk through the valley of the shadow of death. Revelation chapter six records that the fulfillment of end-time activities must be put on hold until the full quota of martyrs have faced their tragic yet glorious fate.

> And when he had opened the fifth seal, I saw under the altar the souls of them that were slain for the word of God, and for the testimony which they held: And they cried with a loud voice, saying, How long, O Lord, holy and true, dost thou not judge and avenge our blood on them that dwell on the earth? And white robes were given unto every one of them; and it was said unto them, that they should rest yet for a little season, until their fellowservants also and their brethren, that should be killed as they were, should be fulfilled. (verses 6:9-11)

Discerning the Times

Discerning the Signs

Once we begin to get our focus on the things that really matter about the end times, we will begin to think a lot more soberly about the times in which we live and will have less and less focus on the sensationalistic approach that many apocalyptic teachers try to incite us with.

Several months before the new millennium began, a lady called me wanting to know what our church was doing to prepare for Y2K. She was, in my opinion, almost obsessed as she talked about how important it was for us to be ready. Her whole objective was that when the disaster hit, we were to be in a position to minister to the folks who were going to be in need. "What a wonderful chance to witness to our neighbors," she insisted. To her, the whole thing was a God-given opportunity to bring in a harvest for the kingdom of God. As people were thrown into devastation, they were going to turn to the church for help and we were going to bring them into the kingdom by the droves. We, like Esther of old, were put in position for "such a time as this"! I had three major problems with her analysis of the situation.

The first problem I had with her scenario was that our church runs a food pantry three hundred sixty-five days a year for people who need emergency assistance, but I had yet to see a harvest of souls come from the soup lines. I suspect that if the Christians did stockpile supplies to help people through the shortages which were supposed to have resulted from the projected computer glitches, our efforts would have resulted in satisfied sinners rather than hungry ones--but very few, if any, converts.

My second problem is that I didn't notice anyone at Wal-Mart asking the people who were hoarding up Y2K rations and purchasing generators if they were Christian. As best as I could tell, the sinners were able to stock up just as easily as the believers were. Hence, I asked the question why this lady and so many others felt that the church was supposed to have the corner on the market of preparedness for Y2K.

But my real problem was, "If it was from God, why did a computer technician or some engineer--rather than a prophet--get the revelation and call out the warning?" It seems that my Bible teaches that the prophets of God are the ones who are to receive the warnings of impending disaster. Amos 3:7 proclaims, "Surely the Lord GOD will do nothing, but he revealeth his secret unto his servants the prophets." God does not tell us to go to the secular analysts and get our predictions. Rather, He promises that He will speak to His people first. Genesis 18:17 gives us a living example when God warned Moses of the imminent doom of Sodom and Gomorrah, "And the LORD said, Shall I hide from Abraham that thing which I do." The stories of Joseph in Egypt and Daniel in Babylon further bolster the message that it is through God's people that the future is to be told. In both of these cases, God gave a message to the secular authorities, but no one even knew how to begin to intorpret the messages; it was only God's men who could tell them that the cows and ears of corn spoke of coming famine, or that the statue of mixed metals predicted the coming world empires, or that the message on plaster in the banquet room was the nation's "handwriting on the wall."

Biblically, the prophets of God have always gone countercurrent to the news media and the secular advisors. These worldly sources may have their fingers on the pulse of the times, but the prophets of God have their ears tuned to the One who holds the future. First Kings chapter twenty-two illustrates this point. All the secular prophets agreed but were wrong; one man stood against the tide, and he was right.

> And Jehoshaphat said unto the king of Israel, Enquire, I pray thee, at the word of the LORD to day. Then the king of Israel gathered the prophets together, about four hundred men, and said unto them, Shall I go against Ramothgilead to battle, or shall I forbear? And they said, Go up; for the Lord shall deliver it into the hand of the king. And Jehoshaphat said, Is there not here a prophet of the LORD besides, that we might enquire of him? And the king of Israel said unto Jehoshaphat, There is yet one man, Micaiah the son of Imlah, by whom we may enquire of the LORD: but I hate him; for he doth not prophesy good concerning me, but evil. And Jehoshaphat said, Let not the king say so. (verses 4-8)

Jeremiah was another great example when he bought a piece of land while the nation was under siege. If he had "followed the market," he would have known that this was not the time to invest in real estate! Yet, he followed the Word of the Lord and proved the secular prognosticators wrong. Chapter thirty-two records:

> Behold, Hanameel the son of Shallum thine uncle shall come unto thee, saying, Buy thee my field that is in

Anathoth: for the right of redemption is thine to buy it. So Hanameel mine uncle's son came to me in the court of the prison according to the word of the LORD, and said unto me, Buy my field, I pray thee, that is in Anathoth, which is in the country of Benjamin: for the right of inheritance is thine, and the redemption is thine; buy it for thyself. Then I knew that this was the word of the LORD. And I bought the field of Hanameel my uncle's son, that was in Anathoth, and weighed him the money, even seventeen shekels of silver. And I subscribed the evidence, and sealed it, and took witnesses, and weighed him the money in the balances. So I took the evidence of the purchase, both that which was sealed according to the law and custom, and that which was open: And I gave the evidence of the purchase unto Baruch the son of Neriah, the son of Maaseiah, in the sight of Hanameel mine uncle's son, and in the presence of the witnesses that subscribed the book of the purchase, before all the Jews that sat in the court of the prison. (verses 7-12)

Second Kings chapter seven tells a story of the time when the Syrians held the city of Samaria in a death grip and the prophet of God spoke a word which totally contradicted all that the news media and high-level advisors were saying.

Then Elisha said, Hear ye the word of the LORD; Thus saith the LORD, To

> morrow about this time shall a measure of fine flour be sold for a shekel, and two measures of barley for a shekel, in the gate of Samaria. Then a lord on whose hand the king leaned answered the man of God, and said, Behold, if the LORD would make windows in heaven, might this thing be? And he said, Behold, thou shalt see it with thine eyes, but shalt not eat thereof. (verses 1-2)

The end of the story is that God did a miracle and released more than enough food to sustain the starving masses. When they rushed for their portions, the king's advisor who had proclaimed that the prophet's words were impossible was trampled to death in the melee.

Because the secular prognosticators invariably turn out to be wrong when they try to predict the future, God actually challenges the rest of the world to try to prophesy. Knowing and revealing the future is reserved for God alone.

> Let them bring them forth, and shew us what shall happen: let them shew the former things, what they be, that we may consider them, and know the latter end of them; or declare us things for to come. Shew the things that are to come hereafter, that we may know that ye are gods: yea, do good, or do evil, that we may be dismayed, and behold it together. (Isaiah 41:22-23)

When God speaks and everyone else is dumbfounded--that is what makes all the difference in the world! Unfortunately, many church leaders have begun to settle for being parrots of the secular trends rather than prophets of God. Joseph was the only one in Egypt to see the famine coming. Noah was the only one to foresee the flood. When Agabus, the New Testament prophet of God, prophesied the coming draught in Israel, we have no indication that anyone except the Christians were prepared for the resulting famine. According to I Thessalonians 5:3, it is when the rest of the world cries, "Peace and safety," that destruction will come. Only a true prophet will be able to discern the coming turn of events. Believers should be the ones in a unique position because of special revelation from God. Regrettably many are busy trying to be prophetic but proving themselves to be pathetic. It could be said that when they tried to prophesy, all they could do was prophelie.

Why? I believe that the answer is that much of the church has failed to live up to the prayer of Jesus in the seventeenth chapter of John that we would be in the world but not of it, "I pray not that thou shouldest take them out of the world, but that thou shouldest keep them from the evil. They are not of the world, even as I am not of the world." (verses 15-16)   John Bevere says it best, "The church has become a subculture rather than a counterculture." We have come to the place that we reflect the standard of society rather than standing out against it. John illustrates his point by saying that Christians are seen as the conservative element in the nation. That means that we blend in with all the rest of the non-liberals. It was not so with the early church. In John chapter eighteen, Jesus explained to Pilate that He had come to establish a kingdom which was not part of the world. "Jesus answered, My kingdom is not of this world: if my kingdom were of this world, then would my servants fight, that I should not be delivered to the Jews: but now is my kingdom not from hence." (verse 36) The end result of failing to be a counterculture is that as the standards of the culture move, your standards move with them. You may be on the trailing edge, but you are still a reflection of what society as a whole is like. A bit less cultured but just as perceptive is the old adage, "If it looks like a duck and quacks like a duck, it's a duck." Much of the church has begun to look, talk, and act so much like the world that we can only describe ourselves as being worldly--a pox which will hinder us from being God's unique spokesmen crying out in the wilderness and His singular lights shining out in a dark world.

    I once read a news article about as tragic loss of several fighter jets and their pilots in a multiple plane crash. The planes were flying in tight formation for a performance at an air show. The pilot of the lead plane lost his bearing and took a nose dive straight for the ground. All the other pilots ignored their instrument readings and followed the lead of their captain to a fiery death. Like lemmings rushing to the death over the cliffs, these men senselessly destroyed themselves because they were so well conditioned to follow their example rather than their senses. As we went through the Y2K hysteria, I continued to ask myself if the church was not guilty of having the same mentality. Had we not progressed beyond the child's game, "Follow the Leader"? Even the great Apostle Paul lived with a constant concern that he might become misdirected and would lead others astray. Therefore he constantly warned the believers to check that his message and lifestyle remained consistent and to disregard any message that he might communicate if it seemed off track.

> But I keep under my body, and bring it into subjection: lest that by any means, when I have preached to others, I myself should be a castaway. (I Corinthians 9:27)
> Holding forth the word of life; that I may rejoice in the day of Christ, that I have not run in vain, neither laboured in vain. (Philippians 2:16)
> That ye be not soon shaken in mind, or be troubled, neither by spirit, nor by word, nor by letter as from us, as that the day of Christ is at hand. (II Thessalonians 2:2)
> For yourselves know how ye ought to follow us: for we behaved not ourselves disorderly among you. (II Thessalonians 3:7)
> But though we, or an angel from heaven, preach any other gospel unto you than that which we have preached unto you, let him be accursed. (Galatians 1:8)

Accurately and Precisely Discerning the Voice of God

We need to accurately and precisely discern when God speaks and what He says. As Paul made his final journey to Jerusalem, he was confronted on at least two occasions by well-intended believers who had truly heard from God, but were advising him to do exactly the opposite of the God-ordained plan for his life. The two stories are recorded in Act chapter twenty-one:

> And finding disciples, we tarried there seven days: who said to Paul through

the Spirit, that he should not go up to Jerusalem...And as we tarried there many days, there came down from Judaea a certain prophet, named Agabus. And when he was come unto us, he took Paul's girdle, and bound his own hands and feet, and said, Thus saith the Holy Ghost, So shall the Jews at Jerusalem bind the man that owneth this girdle, and shall deliver him into the hands of the Gentiles. And when we heard these things, both we, and they of that place, besought him not to go up to Jerusalem. Then Paul answered, What mean ye to weep and to break mine heart? for I am ready not to be bound only, but also to die at Jerusalem for the name of the Lord Jesus. And when he would not be persuaded, we ceased, saying, The will of the Lord be done. (verses 4, 10-14)

Even though the prophets were truly hearing from God concerning Paul's destiny, they were motivated by their own personal desires in delivering the message and advising Paul in how to act on the word. Had Paul not been in tune with the Holy Spirit and cautiously avoided any human misdirection, he could have totally missed the plan and purpose of the Lord. Had he not accepted the sentence of imprisonment, many of the most powerful letters of all history would probably never had been penned and the gospel may never have reached into the emperor's very household. (Philippines 1:13, 4:22)

Another powerful illustration can be found in the

story of Joseph after Potiphar's wife's false indictments landed him in prison. While there, two of the fellow inmates each dreamed a dream. Likely these men did not know of Joseph's record as a dreamer; otherwise they would certainly not have turned to him for interpretations of their dreams because his dreams had cost him his family and his liberty and had nearly cost him his very life. In addition, nothing in any of his dreams had come to pass! Regardless of the circumstances, these two men opened their hearts to their cellmate and spelled out the images they had seen in their night visions. For the butler, there had been three branches of grapes which he squeezed into juice to serve Pharaoh. Joseph interpreted the dream as a sign that in three days the butler's head would be lifted up so that he would be re-established in his position in the king's court. Inspired by the favorable interpretation of his companion's dream, the baker spelled out the details of his own dream of having three baskets of pastries on his head which the birds began to peck and eat. He must have been elated to hear Joseph's interpretation as he said that his head would also be lifted up in three days. However, the similarity between the two interpretations ceased at this point in that the baker's dream was signifying that he would be hanged within three days. The fascinating point in this story is that both dreams had exactly the same interpretation but totally opposite meanings. Each dream meant that the dreamer's head would be lifted up in three days; however, one's head was lifted up in a position of authority while the other's head was to be lifted up in a noose. Precisely the same wording, in the Hebrew original as well as in the English translation, took on radically different--in fact, totally opposite-- meanings depending upon the situations into which

41

they were spoken.

When Jesus came to sojourn among us in a human tabernacle, He fulfilled a number of prophecies which pinpointed at least three different entry points through which He was to step into human history. Micah 5:2 had said that He would hail from Bethlehem, Hosea 11:1 prophesied that He would come out of Egypt, and Isaiah 11:1 in the Hebrew original seems to locate him in Nazareth. Because of all the seemingly conflicting prophecies, many of the biblical scholars had simply thrown up their hands and concluded that there was no way to determine where the Messiah would come from, a conclusion which left them in a state of total confusion. In addition to not being able to discern where He was coming from, they were equally at a loss to understand any of His statements about where He was going.

> Jesus answered and said unto them, Though I bear record of myself, yet my record is true: for I know whence I came, and whither I go; but ye cannot tell whence I come, and whither I go. (John 8:14)
> Then said Jesus again unto them, I go my way, and ye shall seek me, and shall die in your sins: whither I go, ye cannot come. Then said the Jews, Will he kill himself? because he saith, Whither I go, ye cannot come. (John 8:21-22)

Even His closest disciples had difficulty understanding Him when He spoke of His going away.

> Simon Peter said unto him, Lord, whither goest thou? Jesus answered him, Whither I go, thou canst not follow

me now; but thou shalt follow me afterwards. (John 13:36)
And whither I go ye know, and the way ye know. (John 14:4)
But now I go my way to him that sent me; and none of you asketh me, Whither goest thou? (John 16:5)

The mix was even more stirred up by the current misconceptions concerning the Messiah. Was he to come as a suffering servant (Isaiah 52:13-53:12) or a conquering king (Psalms 24:1-10)? Jesus seemed to deliberately cloud the issue when He referred to Himself as the "Son of man." When He used this term as He queried concerning how people perceived Him, the question could have been interpreted as a multiple choice quiz:

A) The Messiah--"I saw in the night visions, and, behold, one like the Son of man came with the clouds of heaven, and came to the Ancient of days, and they brought him near before him." (Daniel 7:13)

B) A prophet--"Son of man, I have made thee a watchman unto the house of Israel: therefore hear the word at my mouth, and give them warning from me." (Ezekiel 3:17)

C) A normal human--"What is man, that thou art mindful of him? and the son of man, that thou visitest him?" (Psalms 8:4)

Jesus acknowledged that it is only by revelation from God Himself that Peter could know which answer to choose when the disciple proclaimed Him to be the Christ (the Greek term for the Hebrew word "Messiah") who is the Son of the Living God.

Three Hindrances

There are at least three major influences which make us subject to the evil of the world. The first may come as a major surprise: theology. To get a glimpse of how theology can hinder our ability to accurately and precisely hear what God is saying, let's climb with Jesus and His closest disciples to the top of the Mount of Transfiguration. Matthew chapter seventeen records the story of how they saw the Lord transformed before their very eyes and witnessed the supernatural visitation of two long-deceased Old Testament figures.

> And after six days Jesus taketh Peter, James, and John his brother, and bringeth them up into an high mountain apart, And was transfigured before them: and his face did shine as the sun, and his raiment was white as the light. And, behold, there appeared unto them Moses and Elias talking with him. Then answered Peter, and said unto Jesus, Lord, it is good for us to be here: if thou wilt, let us make here three tabernacles; one for thee, and one for Moses, and one for Elias. While he yet spake, behold, a bright cloud overshadowed them: and behold a voice out of the cloud, which said, This is my beloved Son, in whom I am well pleased; hear ye him. And when the disciples heard it, they fell on their face, and were sore afraid. And Jesus came and touched them, and said, Arise, and be not afraid. And when

> they had lifted up their eyes, they saw no man, save Jesus only. And as they came down from the mountain, Jesus charged them, saying, Tell the vision to no man, until the Son of man be risen again from the dead. (verses 1-9)

Peter's bumbling about building three tabernacles was as obvious contradiction to the impetus of the moment. First, the point of the transfiguration was to send them forth to the world, not to get them to settle into a sanctuary; secondly, the appearance of the Old Testament leaders was to show their supportiveness to Christ, not their equality to Him. If there were to be any tabernacles built at all, there would have been only one to Jesus--not three. But the real punch line of this story is in the following verses.

> And his disciples asked him, saying, Why then say the scribes that Elias must first come? And Jesus answered and said unto them, Elias truly shall first come, and restore all things. But I say unto you, That Elias is come already, and they knew him not, but have done unto him whatsoever they listed. Likewise shall also the Son of man suffer of them. Then the disciples understood that he spake unto them of John the Baptist. (verses 10-13)

Twice, Jesus has spoken directly to them concerning the coming crucifixion and resurrection: in verse nine, He commanded them not to tell the vision to anyone until after the Son of Man is risen from the dead; then in verse twelve He referred to the suffering of the Son of Man. Yet neither of these prophetic words seemed to register with the disciples. Even though these close disciples had been privileged to experience a touch of heaven itself, their minds were still too carnal to hear what Jesus was saying plainly to them. They were so interested in solving the theological issue of Elijah's return that Jesus' prophetic revelation went right over their heads. The disciples were too concerned about the coming of Elias to catch hold of what Jesus was showing them about His suffering, death, and resurrection.

The other two obstacles to being able to accurately and precisely discern the times are diabolical deception and our own human flesh or carnality. Mark chapter eight recounts another story of the disciples' failure to comprehend the spiritual impetus of the moment. This account is even more startling than their encounter on the Mount of Transfiguration.

> And Jesus went out, and his disciples, into the towns of Caesarea Philippi: and by the way he asked his disciples, saying unto them, Whom do men say that I am? And they answered, John the Baptist: but some say, Elias; and others, One of the prophets. And he saith unto them, But whom say ye that I am? And Peter answereth and saith unto him, Thou art the Christ. And he charged them that they should tell no man of him. And he began to teach them, that the Son of man must suffer many things, and be rejected of the elders, and of the chief priests, and scribes, and be killed, and after three days rise again. And he spake that saying openly. And Peter took him, and

> began to rebuke him. But when he had turned about and looked on his disciples, he rebuked Peter, saying, Get thee behind me, Satan: for thou savourest not the things that be of God, but the things that be of men. (verses 27-32)

The shocking part of this story is that Peter is not only witnessing the supernatural as he did on the Mount of Transfiguration; this time he is actually participating in it first-hand. In this passage, he was operating in the revelation gifts when he discerned that Jesus is the Christ. However, when Jesus spoke plainly to him concerning His death and resurrection, Peter rebuked him and tried to disavow the coming events. Even though it was by divine revelation that Simon was able to acknowledge Him as the Christ, Jesus didn't hesitate one second in accusing Peter when he faltered over the revelation of the crucifixion. There were two accusations levied against the apostle in that story. First, he was accused of being Satan; next, he was rebuked for thinking human thoughts rather than God's thoughts. The Apostle Paul addresses both of these issues in the second chapter of I Corinthians. First, he discusses the diabolical delusion.

> Howbeit we speak wisdom among them that are perfect: yet not the wisdom of this world, nor of the princes of this world, that come to nought: But we speak the wisdom of God in a mystery, even the hidden wisdom, which God ordained before the world unto our glory: Which none of the princes of this world knew: for had they

> known it, they would not have crucified the Lord of glory. (verses 6-8)

Here, he explained that the devil cannot understand the truths of God no matter how plainly they are spelled out before him. He had available to him all the Old Testament prophecies describing the divine plan for Christ's crucifixion; yet, because he was not able to decipher them, he actually fulfilled God's plan through the actions by which he intended to destroy it. Had he had any comprehension, he would not have orchestrated the crucifixion. Paul goes on to say in II Corinthians 4:4 that he perpetrates this same blindness concerning the Word and will of God upon the humans who allow themselves to become subject to him.

The second issue Paul addresses is our carnal inability to comprehend spiritual truths.

> Which things also we speak, not in the words which man's wisdom teacheth, but which the Holy Ghost teacheth; comparing spiritual things with spiritual. But the natural man receiveth not the things of the Spirit of God: for they are foolishness unto him: neither can he know them, because they are spiritually discerned. (verses 13-14)

We can see many examples of this problem throughout the scripture. In Daniel 8:27, we learn that while the prophet was receiving such powerful revelations from God that his physical body was actually overwhelmed, those around him were at a loss to comprehend what was happening to him--much less what the Lord was speaking to him. "And I Daniel fainted, and was sick certain days; afterward I rose up, and did the king's business; and I was astonished at the vision, but none understood it." In II Kings 6:17, the prophet Elisha had to pray that his servant's eyes would be opened so he could see the army of the Lord that was assisting them. In John 12:29, we read the story of the people's response when God spoke in an audible voice from heaven; some said that it thundered, and others said that it was an angel, but no one recognized it as the very voice of God Himself. When Jesus supernaturally spoke to Saul on the road to Damascus, the men with him saw the blinding light but didn't hear the voice of the Lord. (Acts 22:9) We find many other examples as we read through the New Testament.

> And they understood none of these things: and this saying was hid from them, neither knew they the things which were spoken. (Luke 18:34)
> They understood not that he spake to them of the Father. (John 8:27)
> This parable spake Jesus unto them: but they understood not what things they were which he spake unto them. (John 10:6)
> For he supposed his brethren would have understood how that God by his hand would deliver them: but they understood not. (Acts 7:25)

Generally, the inability to discern the messages from God is associated with having a sinful heart that is unwilling or undeserving of spiritual knowledge.

> Our fathers understood not thy wonders in Egypt; they remembered not the multitude of thy mercies; but provoked him at the sea, even at the Red sea. (Psalms 106:7)
> They have not known nor understood:

> for he hath shut their eyes, that they cannot see; and their hearts, that they cannot understand. (Isaiah 44:18)
>
> For this people's heart is waxed gross, and their ears are dull of hearing, and their eyes they have closed; lest at any time they should see with their eyes, and hear with their ears, and should understand with their heart, and should be converted, and I should heal them. (Matthew 13:15)
>
> For the heart of this people is waxed gross, and their ears are dull of hearing, and their eyes have they closed; lest they should see with their eyes, and hear with their ears, and understand with their heart, and should be converted, and I should heal them. (Acts 28:27)
>
> Of whom we have many things to say, and hard to be uttered, seeing ye are dull of hearing. (Hebrews 5:11)

A Vision Whose Time Has Not Yet Come

One other reason given in the scripture that we may not be able to discern spiritual truth is that we are not yet ready to receive it.

> These things understood not his disciples at the first: but when Jesus was glorified, then remembered they that these things were written of him, and that they had done these things unto him. (John 12:16)
>
> Until I went into the sanctuary of God; then understood I their end. (Psalms

73:17)
Then understood they how that he bade them not beware of the leaven of bread, but of the doctrine of the Pharisees and of the Sadducees. (Matthew 16:12)

In Daniel 9:2, we read, "In the first year of his reign I Daniel understood by books the number of the years, whereof the word of the LORD came to Jeremiah the prophet, that he would accomplish seventy years in the desolations of Jerusalem." Daniel had been a brilliant student all his life; in fact, the story recorded about his early school days testifies that he was ten times smarter than all his classmates. (Daniel 1:20) Yet it was only as an octogenarian that he was able to read and understand a message which was recorded in plain language at least three times in the writings of the prophet Jeremiah. (25:11-12, 29:10) The simple reason is that until it was time for the deliverance of Israel from their captivity and their return from exile, there was no need for the message to be revealed. It was an idea whose time had not yet come, and there was no reason for vision to be unraveled in advance of its due date. Daniel 10:1 confirms, "In the third year of Cyrus king of Persia a thing was revealed unto Daniel, whose name was called Belteshazzar; and the thing was true, but the time appointed was long: and he understood the thing, and had understanding of the vision."

If we keep reading in the book of Daniel, we will discover that one vision he received was for a time so far distanced from his own personal ministry that the Lord directed him to seal the message for the time being with anticipation that the proper time for its understanding would come at a specific point in the future, "But thou, O Daniel, shut up the words, and seal the book, even to the time of the end: many shall run to and fro, and knowledge shall be increased." (verse 12:4) A similar command is given to John the Revelator in the tenth chapter of the Apocalypse:

> And when the seven thunders had uttered their voices, I was about to write: and I heard a voice from heaven saying unto me, Seal up those things which the seven thunders uttered, and write them not. And the angel which I saw stand upon the sea and upon the earth lifted up his hand to heaven, And sware by him that liveth for ever and ever, who created heaven, and the things that therein are, and the earth, and the things that therein are, and the sea, and the things which are therein, that there should be time no longer: But in the days of the voice of the seventh angel, when he shall begin to sound, the mystery of God should be finished, as he hath declared to his servants the prophets. (verses 4-7)

The disciples who walked along the Emmaus Road with the risen Lord are described in Luke 24:16 as having their eyes "holden" so that they would not recognize Him. Apparently, the Lord had a specific purpose in revealing Himself to them through the breaking of bread. To avoid spoiling the impact of that revelation, He prohibited them from being able to recognize Him until--with split-second timing--He opened their understanding.

God's Will

God intends for us to seek for the answers to the mysteries which present themselves in our lives. "It is the glory of God to conceal a thing: but the honour of kings is to search out a matter." (Proverbs 25:2) In both the Old and New Testaments we are challenged over having not understood or queried into the meaning of these spiritual questions.

> Have ye not known? have ye not heard? hath it not been told you from the beginning? have ye not understood from the foundations of the earth? (Isaiah 40:21)
> Jesus saith unto them, Have ye understood all these things? They say unto him, Yea, Lord. (Matthew 13:51)

God desires that we have complete and comprehensive understanding. "And he changeth the times and the seasons: he removeth kings, and setteth up kings: he giveth wisdom unto the wise, and knowledge to them that know understanding." (Daniel 2:21) In the opening chapter of his epistle to the Ephesians, Paul prayed one of the most significant apostolic prayers in the New Testament--that they would be able to receive this kind of supernatural revelation:

> [I] cease not to give thanks for you, making mention of you in my prayers; That the God of our Lord Jesus Christ, the Father of glory, may give unto you the spirit of wisdom and revelation in the knowledge of him: The eyes of your understanding being enlightened; that ye may know what is the hope of his calling, and what the riches of the

> glory of his inheritance in the saints, And what is the exceeding greatness of his power to us-ward who believe, according to the working of his mighty power. (verses 16-19)

In what seems almost like an answer to this kind of prayer, the story of Job concludes with his testimony that he has had supernatural direction to speak forth the mysteries of God even though he could not mentally comprehend them.

> Who is he that hideth counsel without knowledge? therefore have I uttered that I understood not; things too wonderful for me, which I knew not. (verse 3)

As believers, we are always encouraged to ask for revelation to be given. However, we must not be afraid to admit that we don't understand and to inquire of the Lord for understanding.

> If any of you lack wisdom, let him ask of God, that giveth to all men liberally, and upbraideth not; and it shall be given him. (James 1:5)
>
> But they understood not that saying, and were afraid to ask him. (Mark 9:32)
>
> But they understood not this saying, and it was hid from them, that they perceived it not: and they feared to ask him of that saying. (Luke 9:45)

As we personally and spiritually mature, this process of discerning the mysteries of God should become easier and our comprehensions keener.

> When I was a child, I spake as a child, I understood as a child, I thought as a child: but when I became a man, I put

> away childish things. (I Corinthians 13:11)
> But strong meat belongeth to them that are of full age, even those who by reason of use have their senses exercised to discern both good and evil. (Hebrews 5:14)

In the same way that God may choose to keep a revelation hidden from some, He seemingly hand-picks others to comprehend His mysteries.

> He answered and said unto them, Because it is given unto you to know the mysteries of the kingdom of heaven, but to them it is not given. (Matthew 13:11)
> And he said unto them, Unto you it is given to know the mystery of the kingdom of God: but unto them that are without, all these things are done in parables: (Mark 4:11)
> And he said, Unto you it is given to know the mysteries of the kingdom of God: but to others in parables; that seeing they might not see, and hearing they might not understand. (Luke 8:10)

Great joy came into the community and the lives of the individuals when the Word of the Lord was clearly explained to the people during the time of the resettlement after the return from the Babylonian captivity.

> And all the people went their way to eat, and to drink, and to send portions, and to make great mirth, because they had understood the words that were declared unto them. (Nehemiah 8:12)

Our lives will be similarly brought to fulfillment and fullness when we, too, learn to clearly discern His messages to us and when we become like the children of Issachar for our present generation.

Even though we may wish to console ourselves with the fact that even the closest disciples of Jesus were subject to the same lack of discernment we are often plagued with, we really cannot find much solace in these stories. If Jesus scolded Peter so harshly, need we think that we will somehow avoid reprimand? But more importantly, we must be keenly aware of the detrimental effect our lack of discernment will have as we make wrong decisions and take false moves.

Three Filters

The Bible is replete with stories of those who were able to see what others simply overlooked or looked at but failed to discern. One very powerful story comes from the life of the prophet Daniel. When the finger of the Lord inscribed a message on the wall, none of the highly educated men present in the banquet hall could understand or decipher its meaning. The professionals were called in to unravel the mysterious communiqué, but they too were at a loss. Finally, the elderly sage Daniel was beckoned. When he looked at the inscription, he found words that everyone present was able to read: "mene," "tekel," and "upharsin"--the names of coins that each person present likely was carrying in his pocket. However, there was one thing different when Daniel read the words: he saw that each word had another meaning when used in everyday usage. Instead of seeing the words grouped together as pocket change, he was able to discern that there was another meaning which could be conveyed. With this in mind, he prophesied the imminent demise of the wicked kingdom. In Daniel chapter five, the queen mother gave a description of Daniel as she told her son why the prophet should be called in for consultation.

> There is a man in thy kingdom, in whom is the spirit of the holy gods; and in the days of thy father light and understanding and wisdom, like the wisdom of the gods, was found in him; whom the king Nebuchadnezzar thy father, the king, I say, thy father, made master of the magicians, astrologers, Chaldeans, and soothsayers; Forasmuch as an excellent spirit, and knowledge, and understanding, interpreting of dreams, and shewing of hard sentences, and dissolving of doubts, were found in the same Daniel, whom the king named Belteshazzar: now let Daniel be called, and he will shew the interpretation. (verses 11-12)

Yet, if we follow the story of Daniel into chapter seven as he continued his prophetic ministry during the next regime under which he served, we will see the story of a future vision which left him perplexed and questioning.

> I saw in the night visions, and, behold, one like the Son of man came with the clouds of heaven, and came to the Ancient of days, and they brought him near before him. And there was given him dominion, and glory, and a kingdom, that all people, nations, and languages, should serve him: his dominion is an everlasting dominion,

> which shall not pass away, and his kingdom that which shall not be destroyed. I Daniel was grieved in my spirit in the midst of my body, and the visions of my head troubled me. I came near unto one of them that stood by, and asked him the truth of all this. So he told me, and made me know the interpretation of the things. (verses 13-16)

This prophet who had such a glowing reputation as an interpreter of dreams and visions--and lived up to it--finds himself at a loss to sort out his own revelation and had to seek angelic assistance in determining the meaning of the divine message. Herein we see one of the first principles we must learn concerning understanding of those supernatural messages we receive from the Lord: if there is any doubt, seek outside counsel. In most cases, we will likely not have an angel standing close by to consult with, but it is fairly certain that God will have placed wise and godly advisors and counselors in our lives to help us through these questioning periods. In Ephesians chapter four, the Apostle Paul tells us that this is the purpose of the five-fold ministry in the church.

> And he gave some, apostles; and some, prophets; and some, evangelists; and some, pastors and teachers; For the perfecting of the saints, for the work of the ministry, for the edifying of the body of Christ: Till we all come in the unity of the faith, and of the knowledge of the Son of God, unto a perfect man, unto the measure of the stature of the fulness of

> Christ: That we henceforth be no more children, tossed to and fro, and carried about with every wind of doctrine, by the sleight of men, and cunning craftiness, whereby they lie in wait to deceive. (verses 11-14)

In the second chapter of his first epistle, the Apostle John assures us that we have an even better source of instruction in the internal abiding of the anointing of the Holy Spirit:

> But the anointing which ye have received of him abideth in you, and ye need not that any man teach you: but as the same anointing teacheth you of all things, and is truth, and is no lie, and even as it hath taught you, ye shall abide in him. (verse 27)

But it is the Apostle Peter who, in the first chapter of his second letter, relates to us from his experience on the Mount of Transfiguration and directs us to an even more sure way to know the prophetic voice of God.

> For we have not followed cunningly devised fables, when we made known unto you the power and coming of our Lord Jesus Christ, but were eyewitnesses of his majesty. For he received from God the Father honour and glory, when there came such a voice to him from the excellent glory, This is my beloved Son, in whom I am well pleased. And this voice which came from heaven we heard, when we were with him in the holy mount. We have also a more sure word of

> prophecy; whereunto ye do well that ye take heed, as unto a light that shineth in a dark place, until the day dawn, and the day star arise in your hearts: Knowing this first, that no prophecy of the scripture is of any private interpretation. For the prophecy came not in old time by the will of man: but holy men of God spake as they were moved by the Holy Ghost. (verses 16-21)

He insists that he was not deceived by other men's stories but was an actual eyewitness to the supernatural visitation on that mountain; yet, he still affirms a more unquestionable source than his own incomparable experience: the written Word of God.

So we see that we have three filters through which we must pass each dream, vision, and prophetic word so that we can rest assured that we are interpreting it accurately: godly counsel by the leadership God has placed in our lives, the witness of the Holy Spirit inside of us, and the confirmation of the Word of God. Notice one additional thing which Solomon shares about the revelatory nature and power of the written Word as he writes to his son in the opening chapter of the book of Proverbs.

> The proverbs of Solomon the son of David, king of Israel; To know wisdom and instruction; to perceive the words of understanding; To receive the instruction of wisdom, justice, and judgment, and equity; To give subtilty to the simple, to the young man knowledge and discretion. A wise man will hear, and will increase learning;

and a man of understanding shall attain unto wise counsels: To understand a proverb, and the interpretation; the words of the wise, and their dark sayings. (verses 1-6)

As he pens this missive, which is to eventually become part of the canonized Word of God, the wise man insists that what he is writing is the actual source of understanding all wisdom and the answer to all of life's mysteries and questions.

Three Responses

Once we get past the deception that would keep us from recognizing the true prophetic voice of God, we must be prepared as to how to respond when we do hear that voice. I believe that our first line of response would be to intercede. As soon as Abraham understood that destruction loomed over the cities of Sodom and Gomorrah, he stepped into the courageous role as a bargainer for their preservation. (Genesis 18:23-32) Moses went a step further and actually put his own life on the line as he negotiated for Israel's destiny in Exodus 32:9-14. However, we must remember that intercession alone has its limitations. When the people of Israel had determinately set their own course and refused to respond to the Lord's correction, the Lord revealed to the prophet Ezekiel that even Noah, Daniel, and Job themselves could not deliver them if they were there to intercede. (verses 14:12-21) Certainly, we can always pray, but we must pray according to the will of God. (I John 5:16) We must realize that sometimes the revelation is only a warning; at other times it, it is an ultimatum.

Secondly, we can speak out. The book of Jonah paints a graphic picture of a prophet whose words--

regardless of his personal attitude--saved an entire nation. I'm sure that Jonah had legitimate enough reason for not wanting to go to Nineveh. After all, this was the capital of the Assyrian nation which had mercilessly razed his own country. The prophet Isaiah described their ravaging as if the countryside had been shaved with a razor from head to toe. (verse 7:20) The landscape was totally denuded, not a tree was left standing, every field was mowed down, and the cities were burned to the ground. All that was left in the wake of the marauding army were the ashes of what was previously the homes of happy families, heaps of rubble on the sites once graced with beautiful cities, and piles of corpses as indicators of the former bustling communities. My guess is that Jonah's only consolation concerning his commission was that he was able to declare their imminent destruction. When the city surprisingly repented and called out to God for mercy, the prophet was immeasurably upset that God relented on His threat. Though there are some valuable lessons to be learned from the dynamic interaction between the prophet and God, we must limit our present discussion to the fact that one prophet's warning saved an entire city.

    Our third line of response can be to take action and motivate others to act. A great illustration of this principle comes from the life of Joseph when he prompted the king of Egypt to become pro-active concerning the prophesied years of drought by storing up twenty percent of the harvest each year during the seven good years of plenty. I must admit that had I been in Joseph's sandals that day, I would have suggested stockpiling fifty percent of the increase. The math seems fairly simple: if you are going to have to live for fourteen years on only seven years of crops, you need to make each year's crop count for two years of consumption; therefore, save half of it for later use. Against all human logic, he only set aside one fifth of the harvest. Why? Because he was following the vision exactly as God gave it to him--and that just so happens to be the only way to succeed! Similarly, the New Testament prophet Agabus motivated the first century church to actively prepare to take care of the saints who would be effected by the famine which he foresaw. An old expression tells us that to be forewarned is to be forearmed. Yet we are truly forearmed only if we believe the forewarning enough to act on it and to motive others to also follow suit.

Probably the strongest acid test of our commitment to what we believe is our willingness to invest in it. If we really believe the prophetic word, we will put our money where our mouth is. Jerusalem in AD 70 was under siege by the Roman army--not just any battalion, but the top legion of the empire. The troops under the direction of Vespasian had the Holy City within their grasp when news came from Rome that Emperor Nero had died. Vespasian wheeled his troops around and rushed home to claim the title of world monarch for himself. In his stead, Vespasian sent his own son Titus back to finish the gory task of razing the Jewish capital. The new commander zealously went after the prize his father had left behind. Jerusalem's desolation was so ruthlessly executed that Josephus' record of the carnage dwarfs any modern horror story's script. Women feared to set foot into the streets to pull in the bodies of their wounded or dead sons and husbands. The streets ran like rivers of blood and the air was putrid with the stench of rotting human flesh. So many Hebrews taken as live captives were crucified that the Romans totally deforested the Judean hills in their ravenous quest for wood to build crosses. Once the timber supply was depleted, the Jerusalem wall itself became a gigantic execution machine with hundreds of victims nailed into its solid stone face.

    Yet, for one special community in the city, historians report a radically different story. The people known as Christians, when they saw Vespasian approach and retreat, remembered the warnings that their Lord Jesus had shared nearly forty years before. One evening He had sat with His followers on the Mount of Olives looking out upon the panoramic view of the Golden City. Before them stood the glorious temple, newly rebuilt and magnificently refurbished under Herod the Great. Constructed of massive stones which defy modern engineers to explain how they were brought into position, overlaid with gold, wrought with the most exquisite handiwork of human capability, the temple rose as a monument to God and His chosen nation. Jesus, gazing upon this spectacle, sighed to His followers that this crowning jewel of man's achievements--this apex, this zenith of human endeavor--would soon be nothing but rubble. He went on to explain that they would have a warning and be given time to flee before the invading deluge inundated them in its destructive sweep. Jesus warned His disciples that when they saw an army encompass the city that it was time for the believers to flee. (Luke 21:20-24) They should not even go back into their houses to gather up their possessions. (Matthew 24:17) When Vespasian's army unexpectedly retreated, the believers knew that this was the chance Jesus had promised for their escape. Dr. Luke has recorded for us in his account of the Acts of the Apostles that the early Christians had sold their possessions and laid the money at the feet of the apostles to be used to feed and clothe the widows and orphans. They had all things in common, providing enough for each person's need and a treasury for evangelizing the unbelievers. So when they saw the prophesied sign, no one was tempted with earthly things--they had none! All they had were the beloved widows and orphans and the precious converts. Throwing their arms around these precious souls, the Christians marched triumphantly through the gates of Jerusalem.

    The unbelievers danced in the streets when the invading armies pulled back, but their joy soon turned to wails as Titus appeared over the horizon. The Christians, unlike Lot's wife, had left no treasure in the city and did not even look back. They marched out to safety, a new life, and a world mission. Because they had really believed what Jesus had said on the crest of that hill overlooking the city, they had spent the four intervening decades investing in the ministry rather than in real estate. Now, they were able to celebrate victoriously while others suffered deadly consequences.

    Earlier in our study we looked at the story of how the prophet Jeremiah bought land even though he knew that the Babylonian army was posed to invade the land, sack the cities, and confiscate the property. In his case, the prophet also had a revelation that the land would be returned to its rightful owner within his own lifetime; therefore, he could invest in property--or, more accurately, we should say that he could safely invest in the vision! For the first century Christians, there was no revelation concerning the restoration of the property; therefore, their only safe investment was in the souls of men. In reality, the return of the land after the destruction in AD 70 did not come until 1948--

nearly two millennia later, an awfully long time to wait for your real estate to appreciate.

Lights in a Dark World

It is my prayer that the church will wake up to the fact that we really are not standing out against the present evil age as much as we like to convince ourselves that we are. I agree with the prayer of the Apostle Paul that the church would truly become "the sons of God, without rebuke, in the midst of a crooked and perverse nation, among whom ye shine as lights in the world, holding forth the word of life." (Philippians 2:15-16) We may be prophets to the nation, we may be prophets to our families, or we may be prophets to just our own lives; but regardless of our sphere of influence, we must be the voice of one crying in the wilderness, "Make straight the way of the Lord." (John 1:23)

Responding to the Times

Where Can We Look in Times Like These?

In what seems almost symbolic, one of my study Bible is coming apart at the seams with a total break at II Peter chapter three. The result is that the book naturally flops open at this particular passage as if to purposely remind me of the Peter' words.

> But the day of the Lord will come as a thief in the night; in the which the heavens shall pass away with a great noise, and the elements shall melt with fervent heat, the earth also and the works that are therein shall be burned up. Seeing then that all these things shall be dissolved, what manner of persons ought ye to be in all holy conversation and godliness, Looking for and hasting unto the coming of the day of God, wherein the heavens being on fire shall be dissolved, and the elements shall melt with fervent heat? Nevertheless we, according to his promise, look for new heavens and a new earth, wherein dwelleth righteousness. (verses 10-13)

Three times in this short passage concerning our stance of readiness for the end times, the apostle uses the verb "to see." He tells us to take notice that TETWAWKI is coming and to determine what kind of people we must be in light of that reality; he admonishes us to look for and eagerly anticipate the day when this transition is to occur; he commands us to look for the new heavens and new earth which are promised as a replacement for the present evil age.

I'm sure that we are all aware that we are living in what the scripture refers to as perilous times. In times like these, it is important that we have a proper focus for our attention lest we become victims of the chaos of the times. We must be like the sons of Issachar who understood the times in which they lived and kept a proper perspective on all the events around them. (I Chronicles 12:32) The question I'm asking today is, "Where can we look in times like these?"

The first place we must look is up. When David was encompassed by a multitude of enemies, he cried out as to where he should look for help. His mind questioned if he could look to the hills as a place of refuge from his pursuer, but his spirit immediately retorted that he must look unto the Lord for that was his only source of help.

> I will lift up mine eyes unto the hills, from whence cometh my help. My help cometh from the LORD, which made heaven and earth. (Psalm 121:1-2)

As Jesus sat on the Mount of Olives and prophesied the fate which awaited the city of Jerusalem, He wept over the city because they had refused to look to Him. Calling to mind the imagery of Psalm 91:1 and 4, He said that He was offering to bring them under His wing but that they had resisted. They did not know where to look to find a way through the perilous times they were to face.

> O Jerusalem, Jerusalem, thou that killest the prophets, and stonest them which are sent unto thee, how often would I have gathered thy children together, even as a hen gathereth her chickens under her wings, and ye would not! (Matthew 23:37)

When Jesus forewarned His disciples of the conditions which are to prevail in the last times, He admonished them that they should look up.

> And when these things begin to come to pass, then look up, and lift up your heads; for your redemption draweth nigh. (Luke 21:28)

We must never let our focus be on the conditions about us; else, we fail to see the redemption which the Lord is ready to manifest in our lives. Paul encouraged us to constantly gaze upward, and especially so as we can see that we are drawing close to the end of this phase of human history.

> Set your affection on things above, not on things on the earth. (Colossians 3:2)

In times like these, we must look up!

As emphatic as the scripture is that we are to look up in times like these, they are just as definite that we are to also look inside. If we hope to be included in the raptured host at the return of Christ, we must be purified and ready for His appearing. Just as the bridegroom anticipates a chaste bride, the Lord expects a purified church upon His return. If we are to be able to look up with hope, we must first look inside ourselves and deal with all impurities.

> Beloved, now are we the sons of God, and it doth not yet appear what we shall be: but we know that, when he shall appear, we shall be like him; for we shall see him as he is. And every man that hath this hope in him purifieth himself, even as he is pure. (I John 3:2-3)

> Husbands, love your wives, even as

> Christ also loved the church, and gave himself for it; that he might sanctify and cleanse it with the washing of water by the word, that he might present it to himself a glorious church, not having spot, or wrinkle, or any such thing; but that it should be holy and without blemish. (Ephesians 5:25-27)

In times like these, we must look up and look inside. It is also scriptural that we are to look back occasionally as we face difficult times.

> Wherefore seeing we also are compassed about with so great a cloud of witnesses, let us lay aside every weight, and sin which doth so easily beset us, and let us run with patience the race that is set before us. (Hebrews 12:1)

In doing so, we see that history is filled with men and women who can attest to the fact that the promises of God are real and that they work in the most dire situations. When we look behind us, we see Daniel insisting that God is ready to shut the mouths of hungry lions. We hear the three Hebrew children declaring that there is a fourth man who will meet us in the fiery furnace. We see Abraham as he testifies that God can lead us even though there is no road map to our destination. We meet Moses who insists that even the Red Sea isn't a worthy obstacle when God is with us. These voices are joined by John Huss, William Tyndale, Martin Luther, Billy Graham, Mother Teresa, Corrie Ten Boom, and millions more who encourage us to keep going no matter what the conditions around us might be.

In times like these, we have to look up, we have

to look inside, and we must look back. In addition, we have to look beyond. Especially in difficult times, there is a danger of being too short-sighted. Ten of the twelve spies who went to check out the land of Canaan fell prey to this trap. They came back with a glowing report about the Promised Land, yet they also reported one obstacle which they could not look beyond. When they saw the giants, they evaluated themselves as grasshoppers. Notice that the scriptures record that it wasn't until after they saw themselves as grasshoppers that the giants began to see them in this same diminutive way.

> And there we saw the giants, the sons of Anak, which come of the giants: and we were in our own sight as grasshoppers, and so we were in their sight. (Numbers 13:33)

In actuality, the inhabitants of the land were shaking in their boots at the thought that the Israelites might invade them. Just listen to the report which Rahab gave to the two spies (Joshua had learned better than to send in twelve spies) who came to Jericho some forty years later.

> And she said unto the men, I know that the LORD hath given you the land, and that your terror is fallen upon us, and that all the inhabitants of the land faint because of you. For we have heard how the LORD dried up the water of the Red Sea for you, when ye came out of Egypt; and what ye did unto the two kings of the Amorites, that were on the other side Jordan, Sihon and Og, whom ye utterly destroyed. (Joshua 2:9-10)

If forty years after the fact they were still scared spitless, imagine how petrified they must have been when the parting of the Red Sea was still the front page headlines on the Palestine Today newspaper and the cover article on the Canaan News and World Report magazine. You see, the ten spies couldn't look beyond the giants to the promise of a land flowing with milk and honey which God had reaffirmed to them at least five times. (Exodus 3:8, 3:17, 13:5, 33:3; Leviticus 20:24) Even though they testified that they had seen the promise and that its fulfillment was imminent, they were afraid to appropriate it. (Numbers 13:27)

The same trap can ensnare us today if we fail to look beyond the immediate difficulties and focus on the promises of God. In times like these, we have to look up, look inside, look back, and look beyond. We must also look around to see how our brothers and sisters in the Lord are doing as they are also going though these difficult times. The book of Hebrews admonishes us that we will especially need one another as the evil day approaches.

> Not forsaking the assembling of ourselves together, as the manner of some is; but exhorting one another: and so much the more, as ye see the day approaching. (Hebrews 10:25)

Although Solomon penned the words in Ecclesiastes 4:9-10, it doesn't take a man with all that much wisdom to know that when two people grab hold of each other they have a better chance of standing when things get tough. In these last days, we must look around and find the weak and hurting ones so that we can pull them close in a strong embrace of Christian love and protection. We often fail to emphasize the prophetic truth that the church worldwide will experience severe persecution in the last days. Nestled right in the oft-recited context of the wars and rumors of wars and the global evangelism of the last days is the not-so-well-rehearsed statement that Christians in every nation will be hated in these last times. (Matthew 24:9, 5:11, 10:24-25)

> Beloved, think it not strange concerning the fiery trial which is to try you, as though some strange thing happened unto you: But rejoice, inasmuch as ye are partakers of Christ's sufferings; that, when his glory shall be revealed, ye may be glad also with exceeding joy. If ye be reproached for the name of Christ, happy are ye; for the spirit of glory and of God resteth upon you: on their part he is evil spoken of, but on your part he is glorified. (I Peter 4:11-14)
>
> Ye have not yet resisted unto blood, striving against sin. (Hebrews 12:4)

In times like these, we must look up, we must look inside, we must look behind, we must look beyond, and we must look around. But we must also pay attention to the instructions on the bumper sticker--in what seemed like a remark defiant of our Christian optimism--that reminds us of one more direction we must look, "Keep looking down!" It is only after reading the second line, "You are seated in heavenly places with Christ," that we can realize that it is a message for the end time. Paul established the fact that Christ was seated above all demonic power as a result of the resurrection, but he doesn't stop there. He goes on to say that we are also seated at the same position of authority that Christ occupies.

> Which he wrought in Christ, when he raised him from the dead, and set him at his own right hand in the heavenly places, far above all principality, and power, and might, and dominion, and every name that is named, not only in this world, but also in that which is to come...And hath raised us up together, and made us sit together in heavenly places in Christ Jesus. (Ephesians 1:20-22; 2:6)

As a result, we are to always experience a victorious authority no matter what attack we must endure.

> Now thanks be unto God, which always causeth us to triumph in Christ, and maketh manifest the savour of his knowledge by us in every place. (II Corinthians 2:14)

> For the weapons of our warfare are not carnal, but mighty through God to the pulling down of strong holds. (II Corinthians 10:4)

> Nay, in all these things we are more than conquerors through him that loved us. (Romans 8:37)

We are to look down because Satan is literally under our feet.

> And the God of peace shall bruise Satan under your feet shortly. The grace of our Lord Jesus Christ be with you. Amen. (Romans 16:20)

In times like these, we are to look up, inside, behind, beyond, around, and down. But there is one more direction we must look--out. I don't mean "look out" as in watch out for danger. Rather, we are to look out upon the world around us because the world is ready for the message we have to share.

> Say not ye, There are yet four months, and then cometh harvest? behold, I say unto you, Lift up your eyes, and look on the fields; for they are white already to harvest. (John 4:35)

Not only do we have a mandate to take the gospel into all the world, we also have a promise that the citizens of every nation will be ready to hear in these last days.

> Go ye therefore, and teach all nations, baptizing them in the name of the Father, and of the Son, and of the Holy Ghost: Teaching them to observe all things whatsoever I have commanded you: and, lo, I am with you alway, even unto the end of the world. Amen. (Matthew 28:19-20)

In all our looking, we must not fail to always look out for every opportunity we have to share the good news in a world being inundated with bad news. Matthew 24:14 proclaims that the end will not come until the message of the kingdom has been proclaimed to every nation. That will only happen when all believers begin to take seriously our mandate to take that message to every nation as we look out and realize that the harvest fields are indeed ripe unto harvest. In times like these, we must look up for our redemption is on its way. In times like these, we must look inside ourselves to see that we are purified and ready for the Lord. In times like these, we must look behind ourselves to see that there are great witnesses to encourage us. In times like these, we must look beyond the obstacles to the promises of God. In times like these, we must look around to find our brothers and sisters who need our encouragement. In times like these, we must look down and realize that the devil--no matter how much he may try to act otherwise--is under our feet. In times like these, we must look out onto the whole world because it is our mission field and a harvest field ready for our reaping.

How Shall We Live, Knowing That the End is Near?

I believe that the microwave was right; these are the end times. But so did the first generation of believers. Many of them interpreted the words of Jesus that many of the ones who knew Him would not taste death until the kingdom had come (Matthew 16:28, Mark 9:1, Luke 9:27) to mean that TETWAWKI was to come in their lifetime. But it didn't. When Martin Luther was confronted with the challenge of sending missionaries to foreign lands, he responded that he believed that the end would come before the men had the opportunity to travel that far and accomplish anything for the kingdom of God. Of course, we know that he somehow miscalculated his timetable. However, there is one important lesson we can learn from the great Reformer in spite of his error in predicting the end. Someone once asked Luther what he would do if he knew that today was to be his last day on earth. He began to list all his activities including his time of prayer, study, and writing. The gentleman who had posed the question interrupted at this point with an exclamation, "But, Sir, that's your daily routine! I'm asking what you would do if this were to be your last day to live." Luther responded, "Exactly. You see, I live every day as if it could be my last." This is good advice for all of us. The watchful attitude that Peter instructed us to have concerning the end time will prove beneficial no matter what time it really is. In reality, TETWAWKI is upon us every day in that no day ever presents the same opportunities or possibilities as the day before. Any missed opportunity is a lost opportunity; any wasted possibility is a lost one. When each day ends, we have seen the end of the world which that day had to offer to us. Each morning finds us with a new set of circumstances to face, new challenges to confront, and a new world to live in. Just think of how much life changed overnight on Black Tuesday when Wall Street crashed in 1929, when the Japanese kamikaze pilots attacked Pearl Harbor, when Hitler initiated his "Final Solution" to exterminate the Jews from Germany, when the Hutus decided to implement their plan to fell the "tall trees" through genocide of the Tutsis in Rwanda, and when Osama bin Laden released his wrath on "the Great Satan" on September 11, 2001. In reality, the worlds we live in are very fragile and can be broken and end at any moment. But it is not only the world of society that can come to a catastrophic termination in a split second. Our individual worlds can come crashing to their ends at any moment through our individual deaths. Every day is the end of the world for someone--possibly the people we are around or possibly for ourselves. Therefore, if we are going to live for the end time, we must understand that living for the end may mean living for our personal end just as certainly as living for the universal end of the age. In this light, we must seize each day as if it were the last one. In reality it is the last one that we have for the moment--and, at some point, it will be the literal last day for each of us as individuals and eventually for the human race as a whole!

He That Hath an Ear

Of all the pieces of literature ever written, certainly the book of Revelation--the Apocalypse--is the richest source for clues and hints as to the end times, but it is interesting that the book opens with a very poignant section that addresses life leading up to the curtain call of history. As the apostle John was confined on the penal island of Patmos, his spirit must have grieved for the churches which he had served back on the Turkish peninsula of Asia Minor. Miraculously, the Risen Lord Jesus visited him and gave him words of warning and encouragement to share with the pastors and their parishioners which he had left behind on the mainland.

Many Bible scholars have analyzed the messages given to the seven churches in chapters two and three as a prediction of the history of the church. They see the church at Ephesus (chapter 2:1-7) as depicting the zealous newly birthed church during its first century and a half (AD 30 to AD 170). The Smyrna church (chapter 2:8-11) is seen as representing the period of great persecution under the iron fist of Rome (AD 170 through AD 312). The compromising church of Pergamos (chapter 2:12-17) is designated as a representative of the period when Christianity became the official religion of the Roman Empire and, therefore, made many concessions to the secular government (AD 312 to approximately AD 600). Thyatira (chapter 2:18-29), at least to the Protestant authors, represents the thousand years that the Roman Catholic Church--in their mind, the harlot church--dominated the scene (AD 600 until 1517). The church at Sardis (chapter 3:1-6) is spoken of as being dead even though it was seen as alive and as needing to strengthen the things that were ready to die. To the scholars who have characterized these churches as depicting various stages in church history, this church stands for the Reformation period when the church was struggling to come back to life (AD 1517 through AD 1750). The Philadelphia church (chapter 3:7-13) which had an open door set before it is seen as representing the period of great mission expansion beginning with William Carey and continuing through the twentieth century (1750-2000). The last church in the sequence is the lukewarm Laodicean church (chapter 3:14-22) which Jesus sees as so detestable that He vomits it up. Unfortunately, the only period of history left to relegate to this church is our present generation.

In each of these letters, the Lord addressed issues which are not unique to the churches distanced from us by two millennia nor characteristic to only certain periods of history. The real truth is that He exposed conditions which have existed throughout the history of the Christian church and continue in congregations today. Those words of correction and encouragement are just as vital for us today as they were when the ink was still wet on the apostle's parchment. In fact, that is why He ended each letter with the admonition that those who have ears to hear must hear what the Holy Spirit is saying to the churches. Notice that He did not instruct us to hear what the Spirit is saying to any individual church depicting our specific pigeon hole in history; rather, He directed us to hear what He is saying to all the churches.

As we prepare to live life for the end times, we must understand and live by the messages which He gave to all the churches. In the following sections, we will explore the gist of the message given to each church. The studies are not exegetical analyses of the actual passages from the book of Revelation; rather, they are messages addressing the specific issues which troubled the churches that John addressed and which still plague believers today.

Ephesus--Predicament of Passion
The church at Ephesus dealt with the predicament of misdirected passion. In Revelation 2:1-7, Jesus addressed this church as the One who stands among the candlesticks and holds the seven stars in His hand. From the previous chapter of the Apolypse, we understand that this symbolism means that He is standing among the seven churches which are to be addressed while holding their pastors in His very hand. In other words, He is very much involved with the churches. This is a powerful revelation for this particular church in that He soon reveals that this church has failed in its relationship to Him. As we read the Lord's address to the Ephesian church, we see that their emphasis seems to be on their works and their efforts to discern any errors which have manifested themselves in the congregation. The Lord stresses that He is aware of their works, labors, patience, zero tolerance for evil, investigation of false apostles, and hatred for the Nicolaitans. Unfortunately, there was one problem which beset this church--they had lost their first love. They had become so focused on the work of the Lord that they had let their focus get off of the Lord of the work.

We can gain some insight into how such a thing can happen by looking into the lives of Jesus and His disciples. In Mark chapter six, we read of a very intense time in their ministry.

And the apostles gathered themselves together unto Jesus, and told him all

> things, both what they had done, and what they had taught. And he said unto them, Come ye yourselves apart into a desert place, and rest a while: for there were many coming and going, and they had no leisure so much as to eat. And they departed into a desert place by ship privately. (verses 30-32)

The disciples had just returned from an extensive mission trip and had come to Jesus to report on their adventures. However, so many people continued to come to them for ministry that they couldn't even take time for a simple meal. The Master realized that they needed a break. He knew that they had to "come apart" before they "came apart," so He suggested a picnic in a deserted area on the shores of the Galilee. However, the plan didn't quite work.

> And the people saw them departing, and many knew him, and ran afoot thither out of all cities, and outwent them, and came together unto him. (Mark 6:33)

As you would expect, Jesus' heart of compassion overruled His hungry stomach and weary body.

> And Jesus, when he came out, saw much people, and was moved with compassion toward them, because they were as sheep not having a shepherd: and he began to teach them many things. And when the day was now far spent, his disciples came unto him, and said, This is a desert place, and now the time is far passed: Send them away, that they may go into the country round about, and into the

villages, and buy themselves bread: for they have nothing to eat. (verses 34-36)

The disciples, on the other hand, seemed to be a little less heavenly minded about the matter. When they suggested that Jesus send the people away, it was likely a subtle way of reminding Him that they had come to the deserted place for a picnic; but now the time had passed, and they still hadn't had their break. The only problem is that their scheme didn't work. Instead of getting rid of the people so that they could rest, the disciples wound up having to feed the multitude.

He answered and said unto them, Give ye them to eat. And they say unto him, Shall we go and buy two hundred pennyworth of bread, and give them to eat? He saith unto them, How many loaves have ye? go and see. And when they knew, they say, Five, and two fishes. And he commanded them to make all sit down by companies upon the green grass. And they sat down in ranks, by hundreds, and by fifties. And when he had taken the five loaves and the two fishes, he looked up to heaven, and blessed, and brake the loaves, and gave them to his disciples to set before them; and the two fishes divided he among them all. And they did all eat, and were filled. And they took up twelve baskets full of the fragments, and of the fishes. And they that did eat of the loaves were about five thousand men. (verses 37-

44)

Since there were about five thousand men plus their wives and children present, the crowd must have certainly added up to at least twelve thousand people. This means that each disciple had to single-handedly serve a minimum of a thousand people. Then, they had to clean up after the event. The biblical record is that there were twelve baskets of fragments, meaning that each one of the disciples collected a full barrel of trash.

On top of the unexpected serving that they had to do for this picnic which had turned into the world's most famous banquet, Jesus commanded them to get directly into the boat and start rowing across the lake.

> And straightway he constrained his disciples to get into the ship, and to go to the other side before unto Bethsaida, while he sent away the people. (verses 45)

They didn't even get a chance to sit down before He forcefully made them board the vessel and begin to row the ship the long direction across the sea. They were busy changing hats from waiters to busboys and then to oarsmen.

> And when even was come, the ship was in the midst of the sea, and he alone on the land. And he saw them toiling in rowing; for the wind was contrary unto them: and about the fourth watch of the night he cometh unto them, walking upon the sea, and would have passed by them. (verses 47-48)

These poor disciples toiled at the oars from evening (just after sunset) until the fourth watch (the last watch just before daybreak). In other words, they rowed all night under very adverse conditions due to the violent storm which arose. Remember that all this was after having catered and cleaned up after the big banquet--and that they had just come off of an intensive ministry schedule which had not even allowed them the leisure to grab a bite between appointments! Finally, they had what they thought would be a moment to relax; but they wound up spending their whole day--and now the whole night--laboring without the rest Jesus had offered them.

Most ministers find themselves--pardon the pun--in the same boat with these disciples, continually giving out to the needs of others. They often, like Jesus' disciples in the above story, are never able to stop for a simple break or vacation. As a result, ministerial burn out is becoming an increasing problem within the church. It has been estimated that a minimum of seventeen percent of America's clergymen suffer from long-term stress or "burn out." In fact, second only to maternity benefits, the largest proportion of ministers' medical claims goes to treating stress-related illnesses. One minister described his burn out as a result of more than a quarter century of tirelessly serving as preacher, teacher, minister, counselor, fundraiser, and administrator that resulted in "subconsciously navigating into the age-old "walk on water" syndrome--the notion that, because you're a preacher, you can accomplish anything."

Bingo! The statement brings us to the core of the matter--walking on water. It was precisely in the context of the story we are studying that Jesus did exactly this: He walked on water. Notice that Jesus didn't seem to be stressed out at all by the vacation which didn't happen. That is because He had a different source of strength. In John 4:34, He expressed it this way, "My meat is to do the will of him that sent me, and to finish his work." Jesus knew the secret of taking a vacation from what He was doing while realizing that He could never take a vacation from who He was. He promised us that we could also come to the place that our ministry is really who we are, not what we do. Notice in Acts 1:8 that He promised that we would receive power from the Holy Spirit to <u>be</u> witnesses--not to <u>do</u> witnessing.

The secret to why He was able to walk on water and not be overcome with the stress of the ministry is found in the one verse we skipped over in our reading. Look back at verse forty-six, "And when he had sent them away, he departed into a mountain to pray." Jesus knew that to be able to give anything to the people and not to exhaust Himself in the process, He must have a renewed source from the Father. He had to separate Himself in prayer so that He would have God's love flowing through Him as a pipeline. Even Jesus Christ Himself was not sufficient to meet the needs of the people. He could only give out as much as He received from the Father. In His own words, Jesus described His limitations.

> Then answered Jesus and said unto them, Verily, verily, I say unto you, The Son can do nothing of himself, but what he seeth the Father do: for what things soever he doeth, these also doeth the Son likewise. (John 5:19)

Before we look into Jesus' little stroll across the Sea of Galilee, let's take a quick look at this great body of water itself. The Sea of Galilee is fed by the upper Jordan River that originates at Mount Hermon. The water from this mountain first flows through the Sea of

Galilee and then through the length of the country to its final destination in the Dead Sea. The Sea of Galilee teems with life; however, the Dead Sea--as its very name depicts--sustains nothing in its waters. The difference between these two seas is that the Galilee receives and gives--it is a pipeline. The Dead Sea has no outlet--it is only a taker. Because it is not in the ministry of giving, it is dead. We can learn a lesson from the Dead Sea: our lives will also become barren when we cease to give into other's lives. On the other hand, the Galilee is a constant giver. From this living lake, life-giving water is pumped throughout the state of Israel to irrigate crops and service the cities.

A number of years ago, during a visit to the Holy Land, constant rains made our trip rather uncomfortable. The locals insisted that we not complain, saying that without the showers, we would not have showers. The water level in the Sea of Galilee was so low due to a long drought that the intake valve for the pumping station was sticking out of the water. Every day without rain meant that the pumping system was taking out water that was not being replenished and getting closer and closer to shutting down. Without these rain showers, our hotels would soon run out of water and we would be without showers. From this sea, we learn a lesson on the other end of the spectrum: we must have a source of replenishment if we are to remain viable and vibrant ministers.

I once read a survey that indicated that the average pastor spends less than seven minutes a day in personal time with God. By personal time, I mean time spent in prayer, Bible study, and meditation totally unrelated to his ministry. Bible study while preparing sermons doesn't count--nor does interceding for the needs of the church. Only time spent with God because He is your lord and the lover of your soul qualifies.

As we've already noted, Jesus Himself readily admitted that He could do nothing unless He was able to pattern it after what He saw in the person of His Father. We often mistakenly think that Jesus somehow knew everything about the Father intrinsically; however, this is not the case. Luke 2:52 explains that Jesus increased in wisdom and stature and in favor with God and man, implying that He had to develop an understanding of God and that His life became increasingly more favorable to God as this understanding grew. The same is true in the life of every believer; as we expand our knowledge of God, our faith grows. This is why the Apostle Peter admonished us that grace and peace would be multiplied unto us through our knowledge of God. (II Peter 1:2) Interestingly enough, the Greek word which Peter uses here means "an all-encompassing knowledge." In other words, we must know everything there is to know about God if we expect to live in His grace and peace.

It was in His private time with the Father that Jesus was able to see and understand the nature of His Father and obtain the pattern for His own ministry. In His personal time with the Lord, Jesus understood that God the Father was concerned that the people were like a shepherdless flock.

> Which may go out before them, and which may go in before them, and which may lead them out, and which may bring them in; that the congregation of the LORD be not as sheep which have no shepherd.

(Numbers 27:17)

Jesus was also moved to address this need among the people.

> And Jesus, when he came out, saw much people, and was moved with compassion toward them, because they were as sheep not having a shepherd: and he began to teach them many things. (Mark 6:34)

He also saw that the Father not only gave the people His living Word; He also supernaturally provided for all their human needs.

> And he humbled thee, and suffered thee to hunger, and fed thee with manna, which thou knewest not, neither did thy fathers know; that he might make thee know that man doth not live by bread only, but by every word that proceedeth out of the mouth of the LORD doth man live. (Deuteronomy 8:3)

Jesus responded by not only teaching them but also began to minister to the people's physical needs.

> And when he had taken the five loaves and the two fishes, he looked up to heaven, and blessed, and brake the loaves, and gave them to his disciples to set before them; and the two fishes divided he among them all. And they did all eat, and were filled. (Mark 6:41-42)

Jesus was so attuned to doing everything exactly like His Father that He had the people sit down on the green grass along the shore of a body of water.

> He maketh me to lie down in green

> pastures: he leadeth me beside the still waters. (Psalm 23:2)
>
> And he commanded them to make all sit down by companies upon the green grass. (Mark 6:39)

But what did Jesus discover about the Father during this night which He spent in prayer on the mountain? I believe that He must have been brought to the revelation that His heavenly Father walked on water and also calmed angry storms at sea.

> And the earth was without form, and void; and darkness was upon the face of the deep. And the Spirit of God moved upon the face of the waters. (Genesis 1:2)
>
> The voice of the LORD is upon the waters: the God of glory thundereth: the LORD is upon many waters. (Psalm 29:3)
>
> Thy way is in the sea, and thy path in the great waters, and thy footsteps are not known. (Psalm 77:19)
>
> Who layeth the beams of his chambers in the waters: who maketh the clouds his chariot: who walketh upon the wings of the wind: (Psalm 104:3)
>
> Thou rulest the raging of the sea: when the waves thereof arise, thou stillest them. (Psalm 89:9)

If the Father could do it, Jesus knew that He could also walk on the raging waters and take authority over the stormy sea. In like manner, any minister who wants to pattern his life and ministry after the character of God must spend some quality time with the Father getting to know His personality.

Let me ask you to give an honest, soul-searching answer to the question of how much personal prayer and Bible study time is in your daily schedule. I'm afraid that we would be surprised as to how many pastors--if they gave a truthful answer to this question--would have to say, "None"!

I once asked a good friend of mine who is the wife of a former pastor why her husband left the ministry. Her answer was straight forward, "In all the years he was in the ministry, I never saw him open his Bible except when he was preparing for his sermon. He preached great sermons with real insight into biblical truth, but he never read the Bible for what it could say to him personally." This former minister now works a very demanding secular job which takes at least sixty hours of his life every week and leaves him too exhausted to do anything else during the few hours he does have at home. He never goes to church and rarely spends any time with his family. His children have grown up and escaped from his life as he recuperated in front of the television and napped on the sofa after his hard day at work. He lost not only his ministry, but also his family--and possibly his own soul--because he fell into the common trap of neglecting his personal time with God. But why would a man of God willingly cut himself off from the very source of his life and ministry? Perhaps we find the answer in the very opening pages of the Word of God.

When Adam and Eve lived in innocence in the Garden of Eden, the highlight of their day must have been the daily walk they took with God. However, that all changed the instant that they ate of the forbidden fruit. As soon as they sinned, they began to try to find ways to cover themselves and to try to find places to hide when the Lord showed up. What had been the most important part of their day became the thing they dreaded and recoiled from.

In our lives, we may not be quite so blatant about our reluctance to meet with the Lord, but the same principle holds true: if we love Him, we will relish every opportunity to be with Him; if we have welcomed other things into our hearts, we will be negligent and casual about coming to Him. For example, if a person is committing adultery he won't want to read the Bible or pray because he knows that he'll run across the commandment that says not to commit adultery and that the Holy Spirit will reprove him for his sin. In similar fashion, the busy pastor can let the ministry become his "mistress" to the point that he will become afraid to come face to face with God because he knows that he is cheating against the God who requires that he love Him with all his heart, soul, strength, and mind (Luke 10:27) with a love that makes any other relationship seem like hatred (Luke 14:26).

Other than Jesus, only one man is recorded as having walked on water. We know the story of how Peter failed in his attempt once he looked at the waves and took his eyes off Jesus. Just like Jesus could walk on water because He responded to the Word of God, Peter walked on the water as a response to the word of Jesus, "Come!" But first, the disciple cried out to Jesus asking Him to tell him to come; he was drawing himself to Jesus, seeking to hear from the Master. In our own lives and ministries, we must realize that we will seldom hear the Lord's voice if we don't first make the effort of drawing ourselves to Him. (James 4:8) Then we must act on and trust in His word. In Peter's case, he began to sink as soon as he began to pay attention to the storm rather than the Master. Likewise, we will falter in our ministries if we move our focus off of our personal fellowship with the Lord. Let me suggest several integral elements which can help us develop an effective personal time with God which will prove to be a life source for our personal lives and our ministries.

First is your Bible. This book is the divinely inspired Word of God. Unlike any other religious book: the Koran, the Pali Canon, the Bhagavad Gita, or even your favorite daily devotional--it is God's direct word to you. This is the word which you must hide in your heart if you desire not to sin against the Lord. (Psalms 119:11) I call it the owner's manual for our lives because in it we find all the instruction necessary for every area of living. Because the answers may not be categorized and listed in the index for easy reference, we need to study the Bible and become familiar with its truths. Therefore, I recommend that the Bible be read systematically. Set a planned program of reading through the Bible so that you have a chance to expose yourself to all that it says. Three chapters a day and five on Sunday will take you through the entire book each year. Reading even one chapter a day--as long as you are consistent--is a workable approach to familiarizing yourself with the full counsel of God's Word. Next, I would rush to say that the Bible must be read devotionally. Yes, it must be read with the accuracy of a scientific or legal document because it is the precise truth upon which the entire universe stands and functions, but it is also a love letter--the very heartbeat of a gracious God for His treasured children. We must read it with the expectancy and excitement that we would read a personal message from our lover, dearest friend, or closest relative.

Of course, the important thing about the scripture is that it must be read with the intent to apply it to our everyday living. Principles, truths, and concepts are no more than good thoughts unless put into action. The Bible is actually spirit and life, and it becomes spiritual life inside us as we internalize it by meditating on it day and night as God commanded Joshua to do. (Joshua 1:8) We must become so full of its truth that our entire worldview and core belief system are determined by biblical principles. We should be so filled with God's Word that we automatically have a verse which rises inside us for each situation we meet.

A clever little acrostic to help us note the proper attitude we must have toward the Word of God spells out the "word":

Worshipfully--read the Word with reverence
Orderly--read it systematically
Regularly--read it daily
Directionally--read it with the intent to follow its instructions

The second element in developing a daily fellowship with the Lord is prayer. True prayer is communication with Him: not just talking to Him, but talking with Him--letting Him talk back. There are many different kinds of prayer and many different patterns for developing a lifestyle which incorporates all of them into our daily prayer life. Remember that prayer is not just a shopping list, nor is it just spiritual warfare, nor is it just a time to speak in tongues; it is a time of personal fellowship with God. Address Him with the respect He deserves as Creator of the universe but with the intimacy He desires as Redeemer of your soul; then listen for His response with the readiness you show to your employer and the rapture you experience with your most cherished loved one.

Faith is the third element I'll discuss, though it may well deserve to be in first place. Without it, it is impossible to even come to God. (Hebrews 11:6) I know that all sorts of fireworks start exploding in our minds when we mention faith We all have pictures and images in our minds of "faith." For some, it is getting great sums of money miraculously; for others, it is seeing diseases suddenly disappear before their very eyes. But let's be a little more down-to-earth if we can. The scriptures teach that we all have been given the measure of faith; and since we aren't all seeing our water bottles suddenly change color, there must be another definition for faith that we can apply to our lives. My personal favorite is found in Hebrews 11:11 where it is recorded that Sarah had faith because she believed in the faithfulness of God. What a wonderful way to understand our faith life: simply believing that God is a God of integrity who will do what He said He will do. Of course, believing entails more than just giving mental assent to a concept; it means banking your life on it! If we know what God has said from our time in the Bible and know that He has said those things to us individually through our time in prayer, then we simply apply our faith and live like He is really going to do what He said!

Books, tapes, and sermons can play an important part in our daily fellowship time with God. However, I have opted to list them fourth because they are second-hand, predigested truth--truth that someone else has fed off of and then passed on to us as a mother does when she breastfeeds a baby. The mother eats the meat, extracts the nutrients, and passes them on to her baby. This is, of course, a wonderful form of nourishment for the baby. Not only is it delicious and nutritious, it is also comforting. However, just as we come to a place in our physical lives where we learn to eat our own solid food, the same is true in our spiritual lives. If you saw Stephen

Spielberg's The Last Emperor, you may remember a scene where the young adolescent emperor turned to a wet nurse for milk. I'm certain that you were as repulsed as I was. However, the Bible says that all too many Christians are just like that oriental potentate--we don't know when to give up the milk. Hebrews 5:12-14 uses this exact metaphor to challenge us to mature in our understanding and application of the scriptures. Just as we would not settle for a long-term relationship with our closest friend through only second-hand communication, we should not settle for hearing from God only through other people's revelations in books, tapes, and sermons.

Perhaps music should not be mentioned this far down the list. Certainly, it deserves to come some place further up the list. After all, David did say that it was with music that he entered into the very presence of the Lord. (Psalm 100:2) It is likely that the repetitive nature of music reaffirms the truths of the lyrics by the same principle that meditation solidifies the truths of the scriptures as we repeat and recite them. Music seems to actually be spiritual in its very nature. In fact, the very origin of music is described as having been incorporated in Lucifer, who was at that time the anointed cherub who covered the very presence of God. (Ezekiel 28:13) So again we see music closely associated with the intimate presence of the Lord. On a side note, it seems that when Lucifer became the devil he perverted the quality of music and turned it into an instrument to bring his servants into closeness with him. Music--both sacred and diabolical--gets into the human spirit and also sets the atmosphere--either for the Holy Spirit or demonic spirits.

The next suggestion I'm going to make may surprise you: bring a pen and paper with you into your private time with the Lord. God spoke to the prophet Habakkuk and commanded him to write down the revelation he received. (Habakkuk 2:2) When you are quiet before the Lord, your spirit man is at his most dominate point, ruling over the soul and flesh. It is then that you have the clearest channel through which the Lord can speak. Surprisingly, many of the things He will tell you will be very mundane--not the least bit spiritual. Don't be surprised if He reminds you of errands you need to run and business matters you need to settle; He is the God who is concerned about your total well being and He wants to see that you are in control of every detail of your life. Jot these little reminders down so that, like a good steward, you can handle them as soon as you get back to your work-a-day schedule. Once He has taken care of all the petty business, He will begin to bring you into His private confidence where He begins to disclose new revelations to you. Mark down these truths for further study and meditation; this reflection will allow you an opportunity to analyze the thoughts and give the Holy Spirit occasion to solidify and clarify the message.

    My last thought concerning spending time alone with God is going to seem rather out of place at first: get involved in corporate worship. The book of Hebrews admonishes us not to fail to assemble ourselves together for group worship. (verse 10:25) In Old Testament language, iron will sharpen other iron. (Proverbs 27:17) We will be challenged and buoyed by others as they draw close to God. In like manner, we will also draw others into the presence of the Lord as we enter in. In scientific terms, it is synergism--the whole is much greater than the sum of the parts. The biblical illustration is that if each of us can individually chase one thousand, two in unison can put ten thousand to flight. (Deuteronomy 32:30) There is also safety in numbers in that we lift one another up if we fall or falter. The element of accountability keeps us from pursuing extremes which can so easily allure us if we spent excessive time alone--even if it is in prayer and study. Accountability also protects us from failing to be responsible to uphold our commitment to regular personal time with God. (Ecclesiastes 4:9-12)

I know that it seems that we've strayed pretty far afield from the story of the disciples as they crossed the Sea of Galilee. So let's go back and finish the passage.

> But when they saw him walking upon the sea, they supposed it had been a spirit, and cried out: For they all saw him, and were troubled. And immediately he talked with them, and saith unto them, Be of good cheer: it is I; be not afraid. And he went up unto them into the ship; and the wind ceased: and they were sore amazed in themselves beyond measure, and wondered. For they considered not the miracle of the loaves: for their heart was hardened.

Notice the explanation which is given as to why the disciples had difficulty: their hearts were hardened. If you will remember, the whole premise of our present study is that ministers are often driven to exhausting extremes because of the goodness of their hearts and the heart they have to serve the Body of Christ. It is amazing that when we get to the conclusion of the story we find that these individuals who had such servant's hearts are said to have hardened hearts--a condition which prevailed in them even until after the resurrection. (Mark 16:14) In a quick survey of the Bible, we will discover that hardness of the heart is associated with not being willing to listen to and obey the voice of God. In some cases, hardness comes from outright rebellion. Probably the most well documented case of a heart hardened by rebellion was the Egyptian pharaoh who repeatedly refused to hear the oracle of God spoken through Moses. (Exodus 7:13, 8:15) The king refused to hear the words of Jeremiah which he spoke from the very mouth of the Lord; his action was labeled as "hardening his heart." (II Chronicles 36:13) Ezekiel accused the nation of Israel of this condition because they were unwilling to hear the Word of the Lord. (verse 3:7) Jesus labeled the people of his time as being subject to this malady, saying that it was a work of the devil to keep them from salvation. (Mark 10:5, John 12:40) Unfortunately--as we have learned in the case of these well-meaning disciples--a hard heart can be the unexpected by-product of a heart of compassion which has allowed its focus to get off target by concentrating on the work of the Lord rather than the Lord of the work.

  The very familiar story of Mary and Martha may help us bring the whole issue into perspective. Martha busied herself trying to serve the Lord while Mary disciplined herself to sit at His feet. Of the two, Mary was commended as having chosen the one necessary thing whose benefits cannot be taken away: personal fellowship with God. (Luke 9:38-42) Like Martha, the disciples and the church at Ephesus had become so busy trying to serve the Lord that they had failed to spend quality time with Him as did her sister Mary. In our passage in Revelation, Jesus said that the pastor at Ephesus and his congregation needed to repent and go back to their first works. From this passage, we can see that there is no problem with works; the problem is the attitude from which the works are done. Remember that the apostle Paul challenged the church at Corinth that their works would be unprofitable if they were not done from a heart of love. (I Corinthians 13:1-3) If the love is restored, the works will become profitable. The Lord also made the promise that if they would repent He would restore them to the tree of life which grew in the paradise of God when Adam and Eve enjoyed full and free fellowship with their Creator.

Smyrna--Presence of Persecution

The address to the pastor of the congregation at Smyrna focused on the presence of persecution. Persecution of the church is prophetically part of the end times. We have already learned that persecution is prophetic of the end times. When I first began to study this topic, I resisted by telling the Lord that I was a "good news" preacher and did not want to bring bad news to the people I so dearly love. He reminded me that if I teach only from the Bible, I couldn't be preaching bad news because the word "gospel" itself literally means "good news"!

The bad news is that the Bible predicts that the church will experience universal persecution in the these last days. The good news is that God has made a provision for us in this persecution! Jesus gave us at least three great directives concerning how we are to respond to persecution. The first is found in Matthew 5:11-12.

> Blessed are ye, when men shall revile you, and persecute you, and shall say all manner of evil against you falsely, for my sake. Rejoice and be exceedingly glad: for great is your

reward in heaven: for so persecuted they the prophets which were before you.

There are two great principles to learn from this passage. The first one is that we must look at persecution positively. Jesus said that we are blessed when we are persecuted. We are all eager for God's blessings--thinking of money, good health, nice homes, and happy families. How many of us have virtually memorized the first portion of Deuteronomy chapter twenty-eight as we have so frequently quoted the litany of blessings listed there? But being persecuted isn't exactly on that list! Jesus goes on to say that this persecution is actually reason to celebrate and rejoice! Perhaps a little look at the book of Hebrews might give us an insight into how we can actually rejoice when facing persecution. In the great "roll call of faith" in chapter eleven, those who had to endure suffering and loss were no less men of faith than those who were listed as ones who saw miraculous deliverances. In Hebrews 11:32-40 we learn something about the differences between them. Notice that some of them were delivered <u>from</u> their persecution:

And what shall I more say? for the time would fail me to tell of Gedeon, and of Barak, and of Samson, and of Jephthae; of David also, and Samuel, and of the prophets: Who through faith subdued kingdoms, wrought righteousness, obtained promises, stopped the mouths of lions, Quenched the violence of fire, escaped the edge of the sword.

This was a deliverance of the body. Others were delivered <u>in</u> their persecution:

out of weakness were made strong, waxed valiant in fight, turned to flight the armies of the aliens. Women received their dead raised to life again.

This deliverance was of the soul. Still others were delivered through their persecution:

and others were tortured, not accepting deliverance; that they might obtain a better resurrection: And others had trial of cruel mockings and scourgings, yea, moreover of bonds and imprisonment: They were stoned, they were sawn asunder, were tempted, were slain with the sword: they wandered about in sheepskins and goatskins; being destitute, afflicted, tormented; (Of whom the world was not worthy) they wandered in deserts, and in mountains, and in dens and caves of the earth. And these all, having obtained a good report through faith, received not the promise: God having provided some better thing for us, that they without us should not be made perfect.

These experienced deliverance in the spirit.

If we look at the whole section in Hebrews, we see that there are four areas of suffering which are addressed. The first is a trial of our faith. (Hebrews 11:36) This area is just a test to see how solid your faith is; it is nothing to be concerned about if you are secure in your faith. The second is persecution from the devil. (Hebrews 12:4) This suffering results from the devil's hatred for those who are doing damage to his kingdom; therefore, it is cause to rejoice because you know that you are doing something right. The third area mentioned is the chastening of the Lord. (Hebrews 12:7) When this one comes, it means that we are doing something wrong, but it is still a time to rejoice because we know that God still loves us enough to correct us. The fourth area to be addressed is weariness in the race. (Hebrews 12:12) This suffering is actually more intense than the English translation conveys in that the term "race" in Greek is the root for our modern word "agony." I once talked with two different men who had recently run in twenty-six-mile marathons. One gentleman who was almost ready to drop out of the Chicago Marathon said that just when he was ready to "throw in the towel," he saw an amputee adjusting his artificial leg. The gentleman who ran in the New York Marathon described how he was able to cope with swollen knees, aching joints and feet, and the experience of "hitting the wall" by his sheer determination to raise money to feed hungry children through pledges he had raised in conjunction with the race. Sounds like agony to me! It is only the knowledge that you will come out better on the other side of the agony that can make it worth the suffering. Three great New Testament writers expound on this truth.

> But call to remembrance the former days, in which, after ye were illuminated, ye endured a great fight of afflictions; Partly, whilst ye were made a gazingstock both by reproaches and afflictions; and partly, whilst ye became companions of them that were so used. For ye had compassion of me in my bonds, and took joyfully the spoiling of your goods, knowing in yourselves

that ye have in heaven a better and an enduring substance. (Hebrews 10:32-34)

My brethren, count it all joy when ye fall into diverse temptations; Knowing this, that the trying of your faith worketh patience. But let patience have her perfect work, that ye may be perfect and entire, wanting nothing. If any of you lack wisdom, let him ask of God, that giveth to all men liberally, and upbraideth not; and it shall be given him. (James 1:2-5)

And not only so, but we glory in tribulations also: knowing that tribulation worketh patience; And patience, experience; and experience, hope: And hope maketh not ashamed; because the love of God is shed abroad in our hearts by the Holy Ghost which is given unto us. (Romans 5:3-5)

It is said of Jesus that He was able to endure the cross because of the joy that was set before Him. When we know that God has a good plan for us (Jeremiah 29:11)--even if we have to go through persecution to get there--we can rejoice. You can't rejoice in the face of every pain--an injury or a sickness--but you can rejoice when you know that the persecution is a part of God's great redemptive plan. This is why Paul can say in II Corinthians 7:4 that he is joyful in all tribulation. The joy of the Lord is our strength and it is at a time of persecution that you need the most strength. Therefore, rejoicing is an absolute must when you face persecution.

The second thing we learn from this statement of

Jesus in which He listed suffering persecution as one of the Beatitudes is reaffirmed in another of His teachings--this one from His last conversation with the disciples prior to His arrest.
> Remember the word that I said unto you, The servant is not greater than his Lord. If they have persecuted me, they will also persecute you; if they have kept my saying, they will keep yours also. (John 15:20)

His message here is that we are not to take the persecution personally. We must remember that no one hates us as individuals; they hate the Christ inside us. They hated the prophets, they hated Christ, and they hate us because the light of God emanating from believers exposes the darkness of their sinfulness. They are not trying to hurt you; rather, they are trying to douse the light which shines through you! In the parable of the vineyard keepers, we learn that the messengers who came to the wicked vineyard keepers were abused and even killed, but it was not they themselves which were the object of the persecution--it was the vineyard owner whom they represented. In fact, Jesus Himself went so far as to ask Saul why he was persecuting Him (Christ) even though all the injuries he had inflicted were actually against the church members.

    A third quote from Jesus gives us a directive on how to respond to those who inflict persecution upon us. "But I say unto you, Love your enemies, bless them that curse you, do good to them that hate you, and pray for them which despitefully use you, and persecute you." (Matthew 5:44) We all have a natural reflex of wanting to fight back at those who hurt us, but we have learned that two wrongs don't make a right so we try not to hurt those who hurt us. However, Christ takes us far beyond this level by telling us to do good to them. Before we react to such a statement, we must remember that Jesus did just that by crying out to the Father to forgive the very ones who were crucifying Him. Stephen, the first martyr, followed the example of the Lord by praying for the violent mob as they stoned him to death. Even more personally, we must include ourselves in the list of "bad guys" who received the love of Christ as Romans 5:10 reminds us that Christ died for us while we were still His enemies. The Apostle Paul, who had the unusual experience of being both a persecutor of the faith and then one who received persecution for his faith, echoed the words of our Lord in Romans 12:14, "Bless them which persecute you: bless, and curse not."

    I see a couple important points concerning why we are directed to pray for our persecutors. The first is that it turns our focus away from ourselves. Without an external focus, we become self-centered in our prayers and develop pity. If you throw a pity-party, RSVP with a "regret." Elijah presents himself as an example of how God deals with those who turn inward and weep over their persecution. When he lamented that he was the only prophet yet alive and that he should just as soon be dead as well, God soundly rebuked him and revealed to him that there were yet seven thousand other faithful ones who had not yielded to the oppressor's threats. (I Kings 19:14-18)

    The second reason that we should pray for our oppressors is that it may actually result in their conversion and, therefore, our deliverance. Paul taught us to pray for those in governmental authority so that we may lead peaceable lives. Although this verse does not specifically mention that these rulers may be oppressive, we must remember that the Roman government at the time of the New Testament was beginning to persecute the Christian church. In Paul himself we have a splendid example of a persecutor who was converted to the faith--a conversion which very likely was at least partially the result of the prayers of those whom he persecuted.

When I was in graduate school, I suffered severely under a professor who seemed to almost go out of his way to give me a hard time. This went on for several semesters. All the time, I was constantly praying about the situation. One day in class, he mentioned something which triggered a revelation; I could see behind the professor into the human that he really was. I caught a glimpse into the window of his life to discover that he was a man hurting from family problems at home. From that moment, I stopped praying <u>about</u> him and began to pray <u>for</u> him. Miraculously, his attitude and actions toward me took a dramatic turn for the better, and our relationship experienced a total turn around. Without realizing it I had applied this biblical principle to my problem and had experienced remarkable results.

Another point from Jesus' teachings can be applied to help us understand our relationship to persecution. In the parable of the four soils (also known as the parable of the sower), He tells of some seeds which fall into some shallow soil which does not allow for the roots to grow down too deeply. He says that the plants which grow from such seeds will wither in the hot sun, and He goes on to parallel these plants with Christians whose lives are not deeply rooted in Christ. "Yet hath he not root in himself, but dureth for a while: for when tribulation or persecution ariseth because of the word, by and by he is offended."

(Matthew 13:21)

We must develop a deep faith in Christ which does not waiver no matter what difficulties may come our way. We must be convinced as Paul was that no amount of persecution can separate us from the love of God in Christ Jesus. "Who shall separate us from the love of Christ? shall tribulation, or distress, or persecution, or famine, or nakedness, or peril, or sword?" (Romans 8:35) We must be convinced of the promise that Jesus Himself is with us just as He appeared as the fourth man in the fiery furnace with Shadrach, Meshach, and Abednego. "These things I have spoken unto you, that in me ye might have peace. In the world ye shall have tribulation: but be of good cheer; I have overcome the world." (John 16:33) We must gain assurance that He personally will avenge us. "But whoso shall offend one of these little ones which believe in me, it were better for him that a millstone were hanged about his neck, and that he were drowned in the depth of the sea." (Matthew 18:6)

With this kind of revelation concerning our condition, we can come to the unshakable position Paul described in Romans 12:12, "Rejoicing in hope; patient in tribulation; continuing constant in prayer." In Acts 5:4, the early disciples actually rejoiced that they were counted worthy to suffer for Christ. They had apparently come to such a very mature relation with Christ and revelation of His plan that their being identified with Christ was more important than their temporal pleasure or security. This maturity is demonstrated in the prayer they prayed after being dragged before the council, "Lord, behold their threatenings and grant unto thy servants that with all boldness they may speak thy word, by stretching forth thine hand to heal and that signs and wonders may be done by the name of thy holy Child Jesus." (Acts 4:29-30) Their prayer wasn't to stop the persecution but to extend the ministry. It is interesting to note that they called for more miracles (God's work, not theirs), apparently because they realized that the persecution was really against Him, not them. Since these signs were promised as confirmation to the validity of the message they were preaching, the prayer that they would continue was a commitment that the disciples were going to continue their ministry of preaching and evangelism!

A few chapters later (Acts 8) we read that the persecution in Jerusalem became the impetus for mission work outside the city and region. Sometimes we mistakenly see this as part of God's plan to spread the church; in reality, God's plan of expansion as set forth in Acts 1:8 was that the message would reach the ends of the earth--not because of persecution, but because of the power of the Holy Spirit.

We have often been told--and I've said it myself--that the blood of the martyrs is the seed of the church. It is true that every time the enemy has tried to destroy the church, God has raised up a new army of men and women to follow Him. But the overpowering truth is that the seed of the church is the blood of Christ. The fact of the matter is that the church grows when men and women yield themselves to the anointing of the Holy Spirit, regardless of the conditions around them. In fact, it grows best under peaceful conditions--not persecution. The point I want to stress here is that the church grows in spite of, not because of, persecution.

One last point we must understand is that we must never confuse persecution and simple punishment for wrongdoing. In his first epistle, Peter addressed the possibility of misunderstanding this point several times (verses 2:20, 3:14, 3:17, 4:15, 4:16, 4:19) implying that some Christians could mistake their directive to disobey the ungodly laws prohibiting their faith for a blanket permit to disobey all authority. Of course, we know that human authorities--whether in the home, school, or civil arena--are established by God to keep order in our lives. It is only when they blatantly violate the God-ordained commandments and prohibit the expression of our faith and begin to persecute us for holding to our faith that we are permitted--no, commanded--to challenge their authority and place ourselves in line for their persecution.

In all these things we have one overwhelming warning accompanied with an even more overwhelming promise:

> Yea, and all that will live godly in Christ Jesus shall suffer persecution. But evil men and seducers shall wax worse and worse, deceiving and being deceived. But continue thou in the things which thou hast learned and hast been assured of, knowing of whom thou hast earned them; and that from a child thou hast known the holy scriptures, which are able to make thee wise unto salvation through faith which is in Christ Jesus. All scripture is given by inspiration of God, and is profitable for doctrine, for reproof, for correction, for instruction in righteousness; that the man of God may be perfect, thoroughly furnished unto all good works. (I Timothy 3:12-17)

In other words: stay in the Word and God will see you through!

Another amazing aspect of our response to persecution is found in Ephesians chapter six. Unfortunately, we often spend so much time in the chapter studying about putting on the armor yet seldom figure what to do with the military gear once we get it on. Notice that Paul concludes the discussion with the mandate to pray.

> Praying always with all prayer and supplication in the Spirit, and watching thereunto with all perseverance and supplication for all saints; And for me, that utterance may be given unto me, that I may open my mouth boldly, to make known the mystery of the gospel, For which I am an ambassador in bonds: that therein I may speak boldly, as I ought to speak. (Ephesians 6:18-20)

Do you see it now? One of the main purposes of spiritual warfare is to under gird the persecuted Body of Christ! We must pray for our brothers and sisters in those secret corners of the earth who cry out and have no ear but God's to hear their pleas, who weep but have no eye but God's to see their tears, who suffer but have no heart but God's to feel their pain, who stumble but have no arm but God's to uphold them, who bleed but have no hand but God's to mend their wounds. These brave souls, like the apostles, rejoice that they are counted worthy to suffer persecution for Christ (Acts 5:41); they, like Stephen, pray for their persecutors (Acts 7:60); they, like Paul, would scold us if we suggested that they take the easy way out to avoid their tragic fate (Acts 21:13)--BUT they hurt nonetheless! And we must help bear their burdens (Galatians 6:2) to the point that it is as if we were suffering with them (Romans 12:15).

It was this kind of prayer that saved a medical missionary from death. He served a small field hospital in an African nation and frequently traveled through the jungle to obtain supplies from a nearby city. On one trip, the missionary stopped a fight between two young men and treated the wounds of one. He then made the two-day bicycle trip back to the hospital. Two weeks later he returned to the city and met the man he treated. "Some friends and I followed you into the jungle knowing you would camp overnight. We planned to kill you and take your money and drugs," the man told the missionary. The gang was frightened away by "guards" who appeared around the camp. The missionary explained that he always traveled alone. But the man protested that he and his friends counted twenty-six men protecting him, "It was because of those guards that we left you alone." When the missionary told the story months later to his home church in Michigan, a member of the congregation stood up and asked him the exact day that he was spared. When the missionary told him, the gentleman said that he recalled having a strong urge to pray for the missionary at the time of the incident. "In fact, the urging of the Lord was so strong, I called men in this church to meet with me here in this sanctuary to pray for you." It turned out that exactly twenty-six members of the missionary's home church were praying for him at the time of the attack.

In the passage in Revelation 2:8-11, the Risen Lord explained why bad things happen to good people. He acknowledged the church's works and tribulations and recognized their fiscal poverty while affirming that they were actually rich in faith. In a chilling revelation, He spoke of the resistance the church has experienced from the synagogue of Satan. All His admonition to this church is prefaced by His identification of Himself as the first and last and the one who was dead but is now alive. This realization of His identity should bring comfort to the suffering saints in that it assures them that He has already faced and conquered whatever they may have to confront. Their victory was assured as was heralded in a popular Gospel song, "Because He lives, I can face tomorrow." Even though this church was destined for persecution and tribulation, they were readily assured that it was only temporary (symbolically described as ten days); even though they may have to endure all the way to death, they were promised an eternal crown of life. Truly death is only a momentary experience which ushers the believer into an eternal heavenly reward. Because of their faith, these believers were promised that they would not experience the second death which is eternal damnation. Because they had been born twice (physically and through the new birth), they would have to die only once. Had they been born only once, they would be destined to die twice (physically and spiritually). These believers, were so focused on the heaven that they were headed to that they barely noticed the hell that they were having to go through at the moment.

The risen Lord promised the overcomers at Smyrna that they would not be hurt by the second death. Like David who could write in the twenty-third Psalm of the peaceful guardianship of God even while death was breathing down his neck, Christians need not fear the process of dying, the experience of death, the judgment that follows death, or hell which finalizes the death of an unbeliever. Death to a Christian is not the end; it is actually a new beginning. In speaking of

His own death, Jesus described it as a change of address. He said that He was going away and that He was to return to bring us to be with Him at this new address. (John 14:1) If we view death this way, there is no more to fear or dread about it than the simple act of moving from one home to another. The Apostle Paul put it this way, "For I am in a strait betwixt two, having a desire to depart, and to be with Christ; which is far better." (Philippians 1:23) As soon as he was certain that he had done all that he needed to do here on earth, he was ready to move on to his new home. In death, we experience simply a transition from one form of living to another. We can't deny that the process of dying can be cruel, but the death event itself is described in the Bible as a great homecoming with an angelic escort into the presence of God where we are to be rewarded with the crown of eternal life.

Pergamos--Pitfalls of Permissiveness

In Revelation 2:12-17, the Risen Lord turns His attention to the believers at Pergamos who were dealing with the pitfalls of permissiveness. Their problem was that they had allowed the doctrines of Balaam and the Nicolaitians to infiltrate the church. By permitting these immoral and perverted teachings to take root in the hearts of the congregation, the church had actually invited a curse upon itself. It was a replay of the Old Testament story of Balaam in Numbers 23:19-24. The Moabite king Balak was frightened by the multitude of Israelites headed toward his country and decided that, rather than doing physical battle against them, he would fight them spiritually by hiring Balaam to curse them. Although the prophet Balaam heard God and was determined to follow the voice of God, he is also perverse in his actions. Balaam initially refused the request because he obeyed the direction from God that he should not go; however, he eventually received permission from the Lord upon a second inquiry. The scripture offers no explanation concerning why God seemed to have changed His mind about the matter; however, it is clear that God was not pleased with Balaam's decision to accompany the Moabites. The encounter with the angel on the road demonstrated the perverseness in Balaam's character when he beat and threatened to kill the donkey. Balaam's discussion with the donkey reveals his insensitivity to spiritual matters as he conversed with a dumb animal without showing surprise and as he was unable to discern the presence of the angel which the donkey saw clearly. It was only after this dramatic encounter that he was able to recognize his sinfulness and was willing to forego the mission. Upon meeting with Balak, Balaam reiterated that he could not speak beyond what God would speak through him. Balaam's first view of the people of Israel prompted a blessing rather than a curse with the question, "How can I curse what God has not cursed?" Balaam's second viewing of the people again engendered a blessing with the proclamation that, as long as God does not find sin in the lives of His people, He will fulfill every promise He has made to them. Balak persisted in his attempt to get Balaam to curse Israel by asking him again to seek a malicious word against them. Balaam saw that God had blessed Israel, and he pronounced a beautiful blessing upon them as well. In the heated discussion between Balak and Balaam that followed Balaam's failure to curse the people of Israel, Balaam reminded the king that he had warned him from the beginning that he would not say anything beyond the words which the Lord showed him to say. In Revelation 2:14, we find what seems to be a missing portion to this story; since Balaam could not curse the people, he apparently told Balak how to get the people to bring a curse upon themselves by breaking the Ten Commandments. The New Testament passage says that Balaam showed Balak how to get the people to sacrifice to idols and commit sexual immorality--exactly what happens in the next chapter, resulting in a plague which killed twenty-four thousand.

The church at Pergamos had the testimony that they had continued to hold fast the name of the Lord and had not denied their faith even though they were positioned at the very place where Satan had established his throne. Unfortunately, like the perverted prophet Balaam, they had allowed the Trojan horse inside their city gates. Even though they resisted their external enemy, the internal enemy was ravishing them from the inside out. Blind to the fact that a little leaven was leavening the whole lump, the church was headed for collapse.

Though we have little biblical or historical documentation as to who the Nicolaitians were, there is some indication that it was a group who practiced wife swapping. The story is that Nicolas, one of the early elders in the church, had a very beautiful wife. In fact, she was so gorgeous that some of the jealous men in the church accused him of worshipping his "trophy wife." In a response to try to disprove their accusations, the elder tried to show his lack of over-attachment to her by making the statement that he was willing to give his wife to any man who wanted her. Certainly he did not intend to actually give his wife into adulterous affairs, but the perverted nature of his hearers made them take his statement literally. To them, such a statement from a church leader was all they needed to justify their carnal desires. Soon, a hedonistic cult was birthed right inside the church, claiming to have justification from the very words of one of the prominent leaders. To complicate the matter, their lifestyle seemed to have gone unchecked and their practices seemed to have been condoned or, at least, tolerated. The situation seemed reminiscent of the similar scenario in the Corinthian church which allowed a man to live in an openly incestuous relationship with his father's wife. Paul sternly addressed this issue with the ultimatum that sinners within the church must not go unchecked while sinners outside the church must not go unwarned. In I Corinthians chapter five, the apostle pointed out two aspects of the problem--the sinfulness of the man who was living in incest and the church's boastful attitude toward the situation. Paul challenged the church to confront the man for his blatant sin, and he confronted the church for their blatant arrogance. He corrected the church for thinking that they were to refrain from interacting with sinners in the outside world but commanded them rather to be careful not to condone sin within the church by extending ready fellowship to sinning members. He concluded the chapter by warning the church to judge error within itself--the same ultimatum extended to the church at Pergamos.

Through their permissiveness, the church had willingly been taken captive in Satan's snare. In II Timothy 2:26, we can read what Paul instructed Timothy concerning how people can be taken captive in snares, or traps. In thinking of the various kinds of traps I have seen used to capture wild animals, I noticed three interesting parallels with the ways the devil likes to capture his prey.

One African tribe captures monkeys by placing a

fistful of rice inside a coconut in which a very small hole has been drilled. The monkeys reach into the coconut to take the rice, but they soon find that they cannot pull their hands out of the coconut as long as their fists are closed around their treasured morsel of rice. Since the monkeys refuse to let go of their little treat, the hunters are able to easily capture them. I believe that the devil and his little helpers use this same kind of snare to bring millions of humans into captivity. If we will simply let go of the things we are holdings on to, we could escape his snare. Sometimes, we hold on to habits which could easily be broken before they become addictions. Other times, we hold on to attitudes which could easily be changed unless they are allowed to remain until they become compulsions. Sometimes we hold on to physical things which must be released before they have us rather than our having them. No matter what the case, we are ensnared unless we learn to let go. We can free ourselves if we simply will!

Another snare which some hunters use is the pit trap where a roof of sticks and grass is laid over a deep hole in the ground. When the animal steps on the false floor, he falls through and is captured in the pit. I am reminded of a humorous story about two men who found themselves in just such a trap. It seems that one gentleman often cut through a cemetery as a shortcut from town to his home. One night, he fell into an new grave which had been dug since he last used his shortcut. After a number of unsuccessful attempts to get out, he reconciled himself to the idea that he would have to spend the night in the grave and wait for the morning when the workers would return. A while later, a second man had the same misfortune of taking the same shortcut and falling into the same open grave. Not noticing the first man in a dark corner of the grave, he set about to climb out of the hole. The first victim decided to watch a few minutes to see if the newcomer might find an escape route which he had missed. After a short while, he decided to warn the man that his attempts were futile, "Give up. There's no way out." But the second man instantly leapt all the way out of the pit and broke all previous track records racing out of the graveyard! It's the same way with many who are held in the devil's captivity--all they need is for someone else to motivate them a little to break out of the imagined bondage which they think to be real.

When someone comes to me with a prayer request concerning something that the devil has been telling him, I always say, "I'm sorry but I don't understand what your problem is." The person will then respond, "Well, I just told you that the devil has been telling me all week long that I'm having this horrible thing happen to me." Then I say again, "But I don't see what your problem is." By this time, I have made the person fairly angry, but he begins to repeat his story about what the devil is telling him. Finally, I cut through the whole issue by saying, "But my Bible says that the devil is a liar and that the truth is not in him. Therefore, if he has told you that this horrible thing is the truth, then the opposite is really the truth. You don't have a problem with the horrible thing that the devil has been talking about; your problem is that you just need to learn to refused to listen to and believe the devil!" With a little "jump start," these people are often set free even without a prayer!

One final kind of snare is the mechanical trap which physically closes on its victim. A rabbit hatch, a bear trap, and a mouse trap would all be examples of this kind of snare. When captured in a trap of this sort, the victim cannot get free without outside help;

someone else must open the door and let him go free. This kind of deliverance can come only from a faith-filled believer who knows how to use the name of Jesus to cast out the demons which have taken control of the person's mind, body, or spirit. Fortunately, Jesus left us the authority to do just that.

> And when he had called unto him his twelve disciples, he gave them power against unclean spirits, to cast them out, and to heal all manner of sickness and all manner of disease. (Matthew 10:1)
>
> And these signs shall follow them that believe; In my name shall they cast out devils; they shall speak with new tongues. (Mark 16:17)

It is always important to remember that it really doesn't matter what kinds of traps the devil may set because the steps of a righteous man are ordered by the Lord; He will walk us around them! However, the permissiveness of the Pergamos church had taken them on their own path, away from the gentle guidance of the Holy Spirit.

To this church, Jesus identified Himself as the one with the double-edged sword. Later in the Apocalypse, we learn that this sword is intended to fight against the Antichrist; however, the Lord threatens to turn it against the church itself if it becomes too perverted. Certainly, He would much prefer to use it as a surgeon's healing scalpel to remove the cancerous infection; however, it will become an instrument of destruction if necessary. As always, the Lord promises blessings to those who will respond repentantly. Theirs is to become the recipients of hidden manna, God's own recipe for bread which contains no contaminating leaven. They are also promised a white stone containing a new name. This stone is likely a reference to the identification stone which fraternal organizations in biblical times issued to their members. No matter what city or country they may find themselves in, that stone was their ticket to protection and provision if other members of the fraternal order lived in the area. All they needed to do was find a fellow member and show him that stone with the special code name etched on it. As soon as he was recognized as a fraternal brother, he would be invited into someone's home for a meal and lodging for the night. Any needs he may have would be generously and graciously supplied. Likewise, those in the church at Pergamos--and we today--who had held fast the Lord's name are offered total provision through Jesus' name.

> And in that day ye shall ask me nothing. Verily, verily, I say unto you, Whatsoever ye shall ask the Father in my name, he will give it you. Hitherto have ye asked nothing in my name: ask, and ye shall receive, that your joy may be full...At that day ye shall ask in my name: and I say not unto you, that I will pray the Father for you. (John 16:23, 24, 26)

To the believer today, the stone with the engraved name is Christ, the solid rock upon which we stand. (I Corinthians 10:4; Psalms 61:2; 62:2, 6, 7; 71:3; 78:35; 89:26; 92:15; 94:22; 95:1)   When challenged by sickness or disease, we can make our stand upon the rock named Jehovah Rapha, the God who heals all our diseases. When threatened by financial lack, we can plant our feet solidly on the rock entitled Jehovah Jireh, the God who supplies all our needs according to His riches in glory through Christ Jesus. If we are troubled, we can anchor ourselves to the rock labeled Jehovah Shalom, the God of our peace. When lonely, depressed, scared, or anxious, we can cling to the rock etched with the inscription Jehovah Shama, the God who is ever present and who will never leave us nor forsake us.

Thyatira--Problem of Perversion

The letter to the pastor of the church at Thyatira (Revelation 2:18-29) deals with the problem of perversion. If we notice carefully, we can see that there has been a progression as we have moved from church to church. In Ephesus, the believers hated the Nicolaitans and worked hard exposing the false apostles; in Smyrna, the church had to deal with an external attack from the synagogue of Satan; although they still had to contend with the external affront from Satan's seat, for Pergamos the real problem was an internal attack from Balaam and the Nicolaitans; for Thyatira, however, their problem was self-inflicted in that they had allowed Jezebel a platform within the church. Unlike Balaam--who, although perverted, was still a prophet of Jehovah--Jezebel was a devotee of the pagan deity Baal. Permissiveness characterized by the church at Pergamos leads to perversion as demonstrated in the church at Thyatira.

First Kings chapter sixteen tells us of the beginning of the reign of Ahab who not only continued the idolatrous traditions of his predecessors but also married Jezebel--the daughter of the pagan king of Sidon--and introduced their foreign religion to Israel. Apparently, Ahab married her for her wealth and prestige. Unfortunately, the marriage brought with it the idolatry of her pagan background. As the story unfolds in the next few chapters, we read of an extended drought brought on by the word of the prophet Elijah. Only after a confrontation with the pagan priests and prophets which Jezebel had set up, did the prophet call for this devastating drought to cease. Upon hearing that Elijah had executed all her priests and prophets, Jezebel pledged to kill Elijah as well, sending him fleeing from the presence of the wicked queen. In chapter twenty-one, we see another aspect of the wicked Jezebel. The story revolves around King Ahab's desire to purchase the vineyard of Naboth because it was next to the royal palace. Naboth, however, refused to sell the property because it was his inheritance which he desired to protect according to the commandment given in Numbers 36:7. When Jezebel saw how discouraged Ahab was over not being able to obtain the property, she consoled him by appealing to his position, "Are you not king?" Once she had seduced the king with his own self-importance, she then busied herself and arranged to have false accusations brought against Naboth so that he would be executed and the property would relinquished to the king. In the story of Jezebel, we see all the elements which Dr. Lester Sumrall labeled as the three destroyers of ministry: gold, gals, and glory. By marrying the daughter of the king of Sidon, Ahab brought great wealth and resources to himself. The religion Jezebel promoted was a form of the Canaanite fertility cult which involved extremely perverted sexual practices. It is also likely that she as an individual was a highly sexual and immoral woman. Her appeal to Ahab concerning his position as king revealed that she was certainly an individual who was impressed with the glory of power and position and didn't flinch at using her position for personal gain.

An outsider, like Jezebel of the Old Testament, had been invited into the church at Thyatira. The people received her as a prophetess even though she was not even one of their own. When she came, she brought with her all her destructive perversions, teaching and encouraging the people to commit adultery and practice idolatry. Jezebel clearly represents the worldly approach to ministry which many churches have welcomed to help them raise funds and develop high-profile ministries. It doesn't take supernatural discernment to see the influence of the spirit of Jezebel in much of the church world today. Churches and ministries commonly make a practice of hiring secular agencies to help promote themselves and raise the funds necessary to finance their visions and dreams--and their lifestyles. I'll share just one example. One minister who was about to launch an extensive media outreach was approached by a promotions company which represented a number of leading evangelists. A meeting was arranged for them to present their proposal as to how they could ensure him a million-dollar return from their campaign. They laid out the program, showing how this evangelist was to talk about his orphan operations in various third-world nations. When the gentleman interrupted them with the question as why they had built the promotion around funding orphanages since his ministry did not do orphan work, they responded, "But these other organizations we represent don't have orphanages either!" They were promoting a secular approach to business built on deception and fraud--and had been successful in implementing it in a number of major evangelical ministries. When the church extends the invitation for such worldly counselors to come in and direct their affairs, they also swing wide the door for them to enter with all their baggage including the perversions of gold, gals, and glory.

Although there were a few in the church who had not entered into what the Lord called "the depths of Satan," the church as a whole had fallen into general perversion by encouraging false doctrine to be taught among them. The Risen Lord's acknowledgment of this church's works, charity, and service confirms that they were busy ministering and doing commendable works; unfortunately, their approach and techniques were far short of commendable. Yet, there remains a promise to those who will submit to the Lord's correction; they are to be given a place of dominion over the nations. While Jezebel and all her children (everything birthed from her influence) are to be destroyed, those who turn from her seduction will be given a place of authority in the world. The irony is that those who are duped into believing that worldly techniques and help them gain a place of prominence are eradicated while the meek inherit the earth.

When God created Adam and Eve and placed them in the Garden of Eden, He gave them dominion over the whole of creation, specifically mentioning the creeping things. Tragically, they allowed a creeping thing--something over which they should have exerted their dominion--to seduce them. They allowed the serpent to trick them by his question, "Do you want me to tell you why God does not want you to eat of the fruit of this tree?" That serpent began to discredit God by making it look as if He had an ulterior motive for forbidding them to partake of the tree. The serpent was able to deftly undermine God's credibility in the mind of His subject. Eve, who had never had a negative thought before, suddenly began to think that God was doing something for His own interest without having her best interest in mind. Instead of demanding him to be silenced, she listened to his suggestions and was deceived by the innuendos of his argument.

For the church at Thyatira, God made the wonderful promise of dominion if they would deal with their perversion. He brought them to a crossroads where they had to choose if they would continue in their perversion and be destroyed or repent and be brought into a place of authority.

Sardis--Probing Perfection

In the letter to the church at Sardis (Revelation 3:1-6), the Lord probes the question of perfection. It is commonly assumed that believers cannot obtain perfection and are, therefore, exempt from striving for it. In fact, that whole philosophy was once flaunted on bumper stickers which proclaimed, "Christians aren't perfect, just forgiven." Such a teaching ignores the testimonies of such biblical characters as Job (Job 1:1), Noah (Genesis 6:9), and Abraham (Genesis 17:1) as well as the words of Jesus Himself (Mark 5:48, Matthew 19:21) and Paul's double admonition in Ephesians 4:11-13. The scriptural context of perfection seems to indicate that perfect people are ones whose actions are perfect because their hearts are perfect. The scriptures teach that Amaziah, for instance, did what was right but not with a perfect heart (II Chronicles 25:2). He apparently fell into the same category as the believers at Corinth who were doing good deeds--and even operating in spiritual gifts--yet their actions failed to be of benefit because they were not motivated by love. On the other hand, David was considered to be a man after God's own heart even though he committed adultery and plotted the murder of the woman's husband. His prayer of repentance in the fifty-first Psalms explains why. His plea before God was that the Lord would not take the Holy Spirit from him and that He would renew a right heart within him. Apparently David understood the necessity of what Paul would later describe as the seal of the Holy Spirit (Ephesians 1:13, 4:30)--the quickening work of the Holy Spirit which constantly reminds the sensitive believer of the validity or lack thereof of his every thought, motive, and action. In spite of the fact that the focus of the letter is on those who do not have perfect works, the letter acknowledges that some believers do meet the acid test--and gracious promises are extended to them. To those who have not defiled their garments, the Risen Lord promises white raiment. To those who have kept His name, He promises that He will not blot out their names and that He will confess them before God and His holy angels. As the Lord identifies Himself to this church, He says that He is the one who has the seven stars and the seven spirits of God--a statement that confirms that the key to successful Christian living and ministry is through the intimate association of the church leadership with the Holy Spirit.

The church at Sardis had a problem of having a reputation of being alive, but they were actually dead. He said that their garments were spotted, much like the statement by the prophet Isaiah who said that our righteousness is as filthy rags before the Lord. Only a few of the people in the church were clothed in garments without the stains of sin and unrighteousness. For the most part, the Christians at Sardis had ignored the metamorphosis of the new birth.

> Therefore if any man be in Christ, he is
> a new creature: old things are passed
> away; behold, all things are become

new. (II Corinthians 5:17)

Furthermore, they had disobeyed the scriptural instruction to put off the pollutions of the old carnal nature.

> This I say therefore, and testify in the Lord, that ye henceforth walk not as other Gentiles walk, in the vanity of their mind, having the understanding darkened, being alienated from the life of God through the ignorance that is in them, because of the blindness of their heart: who being past feeling have given themselves over unto lasciviousness, to work all uncleanness with greediness. But ye have not so learned Christ; if so be that ye have heard him, and have been taught by him, as the truth is in Jesus: that ye put off concerning the former conversation the old man, which is corrupt according to the deceitful lusts; and be renewed in the spirit of your mind; and that ye put on the new man, which after God is created in righteousness and true holiness. Wherefore putting away lying, speak every man truth with his neighbour: for we are members one of another. (Ephesians 4:17-25)

They had failed to realize the power of transformation available to the believer by allowing God Himself to live through us.

> I am crucified with Christ: nevertheless I live; yet not I, but Christ liveth in me: and the life which I now live in the flesh I live by the faith of the Son of God,

> who loved me, and gave himself for me. (Galatians 2:20)

When the prodigal returned to the father's house, there were probably hundreds of young men traveling down the same road. They could have all used a new robe, a new pair of shoes, a nice ring, and a banquet; however, the father only sent his servants for one robe, one pair of shoes, one ring, and one fatted calf. There was only one young man on the road that day who had a heart relationship to the father.

> For the eyes of the LORD run to and fro throughout the whole earth, to shew himself strong in the behalf of them whose heart is perfect toward him. (I Chronicles 16:9)

The Greek word for "maturity" is also the word for "perfection."

> And he gave some, apostles; and some, prophets; and some, evangelists; and some, pastors and teachers; for the perfecting of the saints, for the work of the ministry, for the edifying of the body of Christ: till we all come in the unity of the faith, and of the knowledge of the Son of God, unto a perfect man, unto the measure of the stature of the fulness of Christ: that we henceforth be no more children, tossed to and fro, and carried about with every wind of doctrine, by the sleight of men, and cunning craftiness, whereby they lie in wait to deceive; but speaking the truth in love, may grow up into him in all things, which is the head, even Christ. (Ephesians 4:11-16)

The work of the five-fold ministry will not be finished until we come to perfection. As an apostle, Paul realized that his responsibility was to bring the Body of Christ to this perfection. He realized that the way to do this was to bring them to an experience of the power of the Holy Spirit's revelation.

> [I] cease not to give thanks for you, making mention of you in my prayers; that the God of our Lord Jesus Christ, the Father of glory, may give unto you the spirit of wisdom and revelation in the knowledge of him: the eyes of your understanding being enlightened; that ye may know what is the hope of his calling, and what the riches of the glory of his inheritance in the saints. (Ephesians 1:16-18)

An experience with the Holy Spirit can give us a perfect heart which will make us into perfect men who will demonstrate perfect works.

Philadelphia--Purity of Purpose

Of all the churches, the congregation at Philadelphia (Revelation 3:7-13) seems to be the most spiritually attuned. The first thing that we notice about this church is that the Lord has nothing negative to say about it. They and the church at Smyrna are the only ones who escape accusation from the Lord. The believers at Smyrna were so busy dealing with their persecution that they didn't allow themselves to be distracted and seduced by the deceptions which had invaded the other churches. For the church at Philadelphia, they were so focused on the promises of the Lord that they realized how important it was for them to keep themselves pure before the Lord of those promises. (I John 3:3)

The second notable characteristic about the letter to this church is the open door which Jesus has set before them. They were told that a wide-open door of opportunity was placed before them. Biblically, God's people are always required to go through a period of cleansing in order to venture through their doors of blessing. The people of Israel had to partake in Passover before they crossed the threshold to exit Egypt. Before they could enter into the Promised Land, the men were required to go through the rite of circumcision. Prior to their exodus from Babylon, Daniel prayed a thorough prayer of cleansing, seeking God to forgive every conceivable form of fault: sin, iniquity, wickedness, departing from the ways of God, rebellion, and not harkening to the holy prophets. (Daniel 9:5-6)

Before we discuss this door, it is necessary that we consider the key which Jesus had used to unlock it. It is said of this key that it will open so that no man can shut. This key is also said to be able to close so that no one can then open. I can remember picking many locks to get into cars that had been locked with the keys inside. I readily recall the trip from South Korea when our entire group had their suitcase locks picked or broken open. I also remember failing to get into doors even though I had the keys which unlocked the main lock, because there was a safety or dead bolt on the door. What kind of key could it be that would permit the holder full entrance into wherever he wanted to go and also securely lock up all his treasures so that no one could plunder them? This key is called the "key of David," an apparent reference to Isaiah 22:22, "And the key of the house of David will I lay upon his shoulder; so he shall open, and none shall shut; and he shall shut, and none shall open." In this verse, the prophet is making reference to Eliakim the son of Hilkiah as the one who will receive this supernatural key. This biblical character's historic role is recounted twice--in II Kings chapters eighteen and nineteen and again in Isaiah chapters thirty-six and thirty-seven. In both records, the specific reason give for the deliverance of the city was that it was for the sake of David. (II Kings 19:34 and Isaiah 37:35) In some way, Eliakim stood in the stead of David and held his key. Eliakim's significant contribution was the stance he took against the Assyrian messenger who tried to intimidate the people of Jerusalem into surrendering to his army. Eliakim stood up to him with faith and confidence in God until the Lord caused the invading army to miraculously retreat. Though the scriptures do not specifically identify what this key was, it is easy for us to look back into the life of David and find one characteristic which seems to stand out in his life that could have made the difference between him and any others who lacked this quality. It is likely that we need not go any further than the criteria set for his selection for the throne of Israel. After Samuel had surveyed the seven older sons of Jesse without finding a worthy candidate, the Lord revealed to him that he was looking at the wrong score card when evaluating his options. God made His point that the heart of the matter is actually the matter of the heart.

> But the LORD said unto Samuel, Look not on his countenance, or on the height of his stature; because I have refused him: for the LORD seeth not as man seeth; for man looketh on the outward appearance, but the LORD looketh on the heart. (I Samuel 16:7)

David obviously understood that this was his key to success and determined to keep his heart in a perfect relationship with his God. "I will behave myself wisely in a perfect way. O when wilt thou come unto me? I will walk within my house with a perfect heart." (Psalms 101:2) Even after he sinned with Bathsheba and had her husband killed, the king's prayer was that God would re-establish his heart before Him. (Psalms 51:10) Consequently, the New Testament characterizes David as being a man after God's own heart. (Acts 13:22) He desired to pass this spiritual key on to his son Solomon who was to succeed him on the throne. First Chronicles 28:9 records David's instructions to Solomon that he serve the Lord with a perfect heart. In verse nineteen of the following chapter, we find David in prayer for his son, interceding that the Lord will give him a perfect heart. Unfortunately, the biblical summation of Solomon's life is that "his heart was not perfect with the LORD his God, as was the heart of David his father." (I Kings 11:4)

In the testimony of one of the subsequent kings, we get a glimpse of the problem which also plagued the Ephesian church--misdirected passion. Second Chronicles 25:2 records that Amaziah did that which was right in the sight of the Lord, yet not with a perfect heart. Like the saints at Ephesus, he was passionate in his campaign to stamp out idolatry, yet he failed to passionately pursue the Lord Himself. Because of this he, like Asa before him, failed to obtain what is likely the greatest promise in the scripture: "The eyes of the LORD run to and fro throughout the whole earth, to shew himself strong in the behalf of them whose heart is perfect toward him." (II Chronicles 16:9) This is the universal blessing and promise of intervention by God which can only be unlocked with the key of David--a perfect heart before the Lord. It was the promise extended to the church at Philadelphia.

One other unique quality which we notice about the church at Philadelphia is that, of all seven churches, they are the only one indicated as having any relationship to the Word of God. Not only that, they are twice commended for their faithfulness to God's Word. (verses 3:8, 10) Though all seven churches are admonished to hear what the Spirit is saying, apparently only this one listened and heeded. Like David, they recognized that the key to having a perfect heart was to hide God's Word in their hearts. (Psalms 119:11) For them--and for us--the key to the kingdom is a passionate love for the Word of God.

To those who use that key and walk through the open doorway, the Lord extends the promise that the synagogue of Satan will come and worship before their feet--a promise of turned tables. In the addresses to previous churches, it seemed that the ungodly were the ones with the upper hand; but now it is the purified believers who rule!

The implications of living one's life with a pure heart filled with God's Word could actually be viewed more like a combination to a lock rather than one simple key. I find a list of nine principles played out in Divid's life that spell out the words "David's Key." These nine qualities are the fruit of a pure heart motivated by a sincere love for the Word of God.

D--Do it God's Way

One important key which David learned was that he had to do things God's way. When he realized that he needed the blessing of the Ark of the Covenant in his royal city of Jerusalem, he went with a crew of men to bring it back. Following the pattern of the Philistines, they placed the Ark on an oxcart as he had seen the Philistines do. However, when the Ark tipped over as the cart jostled down the road, Uzza was struck dead for his good-intentioned deed of trying to stop the Ark from tumbling to the ground. David realized that more than an ox had stumbled that day; he, too, had stumbled when he failed to follow God's prescribed way of transporting the Ark. God had made no secret of His prescribed method of handling the sacred chest--it was spelled out explicitly in Exodus 25:14. All David needed to do was to read the book and follow its directions. When he did, he successfully brought blessing to his house.

A--Avoid Carnality

One of the black pages in David's biography is the story of his dealing with his son Absalom. In fact, it might be said that David's actions were a litany of stupidity. First of all, Absalom's sister Tamar was raped by her half-brother Amnon, but the father took no corrective or restorative action. He simply acted as if nothing had happened. Even though his father brushed the matter under the carpet, Absalom was not so easy to forget. Inside him, the incident festered and seethed until he had to take revenge. Soon, the sexual predator fell prey to the avenger. Even though David had turned a blind eye to the molestation of his daughter, he could not let murder go unjudged; therefore, he exiled the culprit and kept him estranged for many years. Yes, it was punitive action, but it failed to be a corrective measure. Finally, at the urging of his trusted counsel, David allowed Absalom to return to Jerusalem. Unfortunately, he did not allow or pursue reconciliation in that he never even permitted Absalom to show his face in the king's presence.

Absalom busied himself just outside his father's field of vision and began to undermine the king's authority in the hearts of the subjects. By making himself accessible to those who failed to get an audience with the king, Absalom began to win the confidence of the people. Before long, he had enough of a following that he felt confident in staging a revolution. Again, David acted foolishly by abandoning his position of authority and fleeing from Jerusalem. Immediately, Absalom took over his father's throne and slept with his concubines in the public vision. When David did eventually turn to fight against and defeat the insurgent, he wept over the death of his son. So inconsistent with the years of deliberate refusal of the son who would have sought reconciliation, David now mourned the death of this same son who had become his declared enemy. Rather than celebrating the victory and rejoicing in the restoration of the kingdom, he lamented the death of the one who had disrupted the peace. Again, his foolish actions undermined his own authority in the eyes of those who had fought with and for him and all who were to be subject to his rule.

The point here is that carnality and stupidity will undo our victory.

V--Value the Lord

One of the last episodes in the life of King David was his unwise decision to count the army of Israel. The same man who had boasted that--even though others put their confidence in horses, chariots, and foot soldiers--he would remember the name of the Lord as his source of victory now faltered in his old age and asked for a census of his military might. A plague was sent as judgment for blatant violation of trust. As the scourge swept through the land, the death angel eventually arrived at David's beloved city of Jerusalem. When he saw the sword of doom stretched out against his capital, David ascended to the top of Mt. Moriah where hundreds of years before Abraham had offered Isaac. On that sacred precipice, David determined to make a peace offering to God. The man who had a threshing floor on the pinnacle offered David the land, the wood for the altar, and his ox for a sacrifice, but David refused. When he insisted, "I will not offer anything to my God that cost me nothing," David demonstrated one of the great scriptural truths to victory: we must be givers and tithers in order to expect that the devourer be rebuked on our behalf and that the windows of God's blessings be open.

I--Instill a Vision of Victory

When David started putting together his team of men who were to work with him to bring about his acquisition of the kingdom, he wound up with a congregation of misfits, debtors, and failures. David welcomed these outcasts into a cave at Adulam where he molded them into his band of four hundred mighty warriors. He had found another major key to success; he had learned how to pick up the pieces and keep going. It has been said that you can't unscramble eggs, but you can take the broken Humpty Dumpty of life and make a winner of a soufflé! Remember: if life hands you a lemon, make lemonade. David believed that every failure was only a success waiting to manifest itself.

D--Don't Quit

Upon returning from a battle against the Philistines, David and his men found that their headquarters town of Ziklag had been raided. The enemy had taken all that they wanted and burned the rest! David's men compounded his distress when they threatened to kill him because he had led them into battle leaving the home base unprotected. In his hour of utter dejection, David turned to the Lord for inspiration and instruction. The Lord told him to pursue the raiders even though he and his men were exhausted from the battle and the journey. Just when they had no more energy to expend, the Lord told them to pursue the enemy and to recover all. They did pursue, and they did recover everything that they had lost.

    Here again, we see another of the principles of victory in David's life: he refused to give up. Dr. Lester Sumrall produced a tape based on his life's story called "I Did Not Quit." On the tape, he recounted time after time when he was faced with insurmountable barriers and unbeatable odds, but he simply kept on trying until God honored his efforts and gave him outstanding victory. The great statesman Winston Churchill concurred when he was asked to speak at a college graduation. His speech consisted of only one line repeated three times. He growled at the young degree candidates, commanding them, "Never give up!" A second and a third time, he repeated his command until he was sure that he had gotten his message across to the young men before him; then he sat down and waited to make sure that the message had gotten inside them. I'm sure that God is calling out that same injunction to us today, "Never give up; don't quit; pursue even when you don't think that you have any strength left--you will recover all!"

S--Size up Your Enemy

When David had come into his rightful place as king, he realized that there would be tremendous political, spiritual, and military advantages in locating the nation's capital in Jerusalem. However, the city was a Jebusite stronghold with deep ravines on three sides, denying an attack approach. In fact, the Jebusites boasted that their city was so naturally well protected that they only needed the blind and the lame soldiers to protect it. David and his men devised a plan to take the city by entering through the water system and capturing the city from the inside out. David was able to conquer because he sized up his enemy and saw that he was nothing as formidable as might first be imagined. Once he got beyond the wall, he found that his opponents were barely able to fight against him. I'm convinced that the same thing is true in all our struggles--actually, Satan is already a defeated foe; Christ stripped him of all his armaments some twenty centuries ago. All we have to do is get beyond the stronghold of our minds that makes us see him as such a looming villain.

K--Keep What's Yours

David had courage to fight a giant because he had already fought a lion and a bear--and had won. The reason he was willing to take on the predators was that they had taken something that belonged to him-- his sheep. Because he knew that the sheep were rightfully his and that the beasts of prey were violating his property rights, the young shepherd boy was bold to go reclaim what was his. When the Philistine giant made claims against the people of Israel, this adolescent rose up with an uncommon determination. He knew that it was Israel's covenant from God to own this land, and the uncircumcised (signifying that they were not under a covenant with Jehovah) enemy were wrongfully violating the Jews' legal privileges. If he could take back what the four-footed predators had stolen, David was confident that he could reclaim his covenant possession from these two-footed predators.

The army of Saul had stood powerless for forty days before Goliath's threats; they had not perceived the challenge in the same way that David did. Notice in the story in I Samuel chapter seventeen that they are always referred to as being the men of Saul or the army of Israel. It was only David who called them the army of the living God. This difference in perception of identity made all the difference in the world. For us to have victory, we must realize that we are covenant people and we must understand what our rights as covenant people are. When we are denied anything that is ours in the covenant, we must realize that the enemy is stealing from us; and we, like David, must go into action to reclaim our rightful possessions. Health, prosperity, household salvation, peace, joy, and all the other benefits of the cross are ours if we do not default and let the devourer rob them from us. David knew what was his and took possession--so can we.

E--Empty Yourself of Sin

Possibly, David's biggest challenge was the girl next door. We all know the story of how he caught a glimpse of her bathing and wound up committing adultery with her. The resulting pregnancy drove him to arrange the death of Bathsheba's husband so that he could take the woman as his wife in an attempt to cover up the crime. David tried to hide his sin, but he eventually had to face it. When he did, he dealt with it by genuine heart-felt repentance and prayer. Here is David's greatest key to victory: a heart after the heart of

God. When he failed God, he shared the heartbreak that God Himself felt. As long as we are sensitive to the emotion of the Father, we'll always be on the road to victory. A good man may fall seven times, but he always gets up again! (Proverbs 24:16)

Psalm chapter fifty-one has long been recognized as the prayer that David prayed after this tragic fall. In it we see all the elements that will keep us sensitive to the heart of God--and make us candidates for great victory.

Y--Yield to God's Timing

The position of king over Israel was promised to the young shepherd boy, but it took many years for that prophecy to be fulfilled. As the time for his exaltation began to unfold, the ruling King Saul opposed him more and more violently. David was pursued like a common criminal; he had to hole up in the desert and hide in caves. Twice during this time as a fugitive, the Lord delivered his opponent into David's hand. In both cases, it could have been the king's head that David carried away, but David acted on a higher principle than human revenge and opportunism. He knew that he could not take matters into his own hands if he was genuinely expecting God to be his deliverer. David decided to stand still and let God prove Himself in giving the kingdom to him. A major plateau to achieve when reaching out to claim all that God has provided for us is to remember that God will fight the victorious battle. We are to simply practice patiently waiting for Him to do His deliverance.

Jesus promised to use the key of David to open the doors of the world to the Philadelphian church. The history of the Christian church is marked by many revivals in which entire cities, countries, and people groups have responded to the gospel en mass. One such historic moment occurred in AD 723 when St. Boniface challenged the Germans to accept Christ. To prove that Jesus--not their pagan deity Thor--was the true God, the missionary took an axe and began to chop away at a mighty oak tree which the local people believed to be the dwelling place of their god of thunder and lightning. As the crowd cowered back expecting Thor to retaliate with a deadly bolt to defend his honor, Boniface continued to strike the tree until it came crashing to the ground. After this obvious validation of the Christian faith, the entire population converted and took the wood from the monstrous tree to build a chapel. During the first half of the sixteenth century, Francis Xavier turned entire communities in India and Japan to the Christian faith when he miraculously began to preach in their native tongues without ever having studied these languages.

More contemporary stories include a number of mass conversions which took place in the twentieth century. Following World War II, entire tribes of aboriginals in the Pacific islands turned to Christ when missionaries landed airplanes on their remote atolls. The story behind the conversions was that these islanders had never seen planes until they witnessed fighter planes flying over during the Pacific campaign. Many times the pilots of these aircraft would jettison cargo which fell within reach of the natives. To them, these were gifts which the gods were dropping from the sky.   When these heavenly visitations suddenly ceased, the tribal people had no idea that the war had ended; for that matter, they still did not even know that there was a war in progress. As they prayed for the gods to favor them with more visitations and more gifts, a cultish belief arose that the gods would someday return--an anticipation which they perceived as being fulfilled with the arrival of the missionaries. When the missionaries told them of Jesus, the people were primed for the message and readily received it.

The account of the conversion of another entire tribal group centers around the introduction of a metal axe head to a Stone Age culture. When the courageous young missionary paddled the canoe containing his wife and two small children to shore in headhunter territory, the natives hid among the bushes determining when was the best time to stage their attack. As they lingered, the cannibals were amazed to see the gentleman fell a tree within minutes as he started to gather materials to build a home for his family. These primitive people who had missed the advancements of the past three millennia felt as if they had just witnessed a miracle since they were accustomed to spending hours and even days chopping down a tree with their stone axes. Their awe of this man's magical power led to respect for his message and acceptance of his God.

In the Solomon Islands, two young missionaries were captured by a bloodthirsty tribe and sentenced to death for trespassing on their territory. Since the king of the people happened to be seriously ill, the execution was postponed as the people focused all their energy and attention on the ailing monarch. When all the magical incantations of their shamans failed to revive the king, the missionaries were allowed to present their message and pray for him. Immediately after their prayers, the king died. As you might guess, this was not a plus for the evangelists. However, the king suddenly revived and sat up on his mat long enough to tell the people about his death experience and to confirm that what the missionaries had said was true. With the final admonition to his people that they should listen to and believe these foreigners, he fell back on his mat and died again. Instantly, the prisoners were released and welcomed among the people. Their message was heartily accepted and the entire populace became believers.

Two more accounts of massive revivals come from the islands of the Philippines. A nation-changing movement swept the country after Dr. Lester Sumrall went into Bilibid Prison and cast the devil out of a young girl who was manifesting physical bite marks made by an unseen entity; she was literally being bitten by demons. Within six weeks, one hundred and fifty thousand conversions and innumerable healings were registered. It took weeks to baptize all the new believers. A more isolated example comes from a remote village where the resident witchdoctor challenged the newcomer missionary, claiming that there could only be one spiritual leader in the area. He proposed a contest to see which one possessed more spiritual power with the understanding that the one who failed the test would pack up and leave. A large stage was erected so that all the village could witness the match. The missionary, unsure as to how to proceed, invited the witchdoctor to go first. To her amazement, the witchdoctor lay down on the stage and began to levitate. Being considerably overweight, she was sure that floating in the air was out of the question for her. When she questioned the Lord as to whether she should concede and start packing her bags to leave the village, the Lord impressed upon her that she was not to leave; instead, she was to prove her superior spiritual authority. A very clear impression was to push the floating witchdoctor back to the ground, so she gathered her skirt around her leg and raised her foot in order to plant her heel firmly in his belly. Taking advantage of her extra pounds, she slammed him to the floor and yelled to the spirit inside him to come out. Once the man was delivered, he immediately offered to leave town; however, the missionary persuaded him to stay on the condition that he would accept Christ. Not only did he respond to her message, but the entire village also followed. The former witchdoctor became the mayor and the missionary became the pastor as the entire community became one large Christian neighborhood with everyone as baptized members of the same church.

A little white-haired Indian man had been trying year after year to evangelize his remote village in Tamil Nadu State in southern India. Yet, his Hindu neighbors' hearts and ears were closed. Finally, at an evangelism training conference in the city of Madras (now known as Chennai), he learned the principles of the Great Commission that signs and wonders should accompany the proclamation of the kingdom. Returning to his village with a new power from his new relationship with the Holy Spirit, he found that an old lady in the village had been gored by a water buffalo. Laying his hands on her, he commanded that she be totally healed. Instantly, her crippled legs received strength and her mangled body was straightened. Since the whole village had seen the woman's condition after the attack and then saw her miraculous recovery, everyone suddenly believed that the old man's message was real. The village that had rejected his testimony year after year was converted overnight.

As we examine all these accounts, there is one major point which is consistent throughout--a miraculous catalyst to the revival. This is also a consistent biblical pattern of evangelism. Miraculous acts at the hands of Daniel resulted in empire-wide decrees from the ruling monarchs themselves that the entire population must reverence the God of Daniel. (verses 4:1-37, 6:25-27) When Jesus sent His disciples out, He commanded them to accompany their acclamation of the kingdom with demonstration of its presence, "Go preach saying, 'The kingdom of heaven is at hand.' Heal the sick, cleanse the lepers, raise the dead, cast out devils: freely ye have received, freely give." (Matthew 10:7-8) He added that even the citizens of Sodom would have repented had they been presented with a message confirmed with manifestations. (Matthew 10:15, 11:23-24, Mark 6:11, Luke 10:12) When He gave His disciples the Great Commission, He ordered them to remain in Jerusalem until they were endued with the power of the Holy Spirit so that they would be able to confirm their message with signs and wonders. (Luke 24:49, Mark 16:17) The book of Acts records abundant examples of miraculous acts resulting in mass conversions: supernatural tongues on the day of Pentecost, the healing of the lame man at the temple gate, miraculous healings and deliverances in Samaria, the raising of Dorcus from the dead, an angelic visit to Cornelius, and Paul's miraculous protection from a venomous snake bite and the healing of Publius' father on the island of Malta. In fact, the Apostle Paul declares that having signs and wonders in conjunction with his preaching was his modi operandorum and that this combination of miracle and message had allowed him to fully saturate his targeted region. "Through mighty signs and wonders, by the power of the Spirit of God; so that from Jerusalem, and round about unto Illyricum, I have fully preached the gospel of Christ…But now having no more place in these parts, and having a great desire these many years to come unto you." (Romans 15:19-23) In his letter to the Corinthian church, he emphasized that he had come to them with the power of God as well as with God's powerful message. "And my speech and my preaching was not with enticing words of man's wisdom, but in demonstration of the Spirit and of power." (I Corinthians 2:4) Perhaps his ministry in this particular city was particularly marked with miraculous signs and wonders because it followed immediately upon the heels of a rather unfruitful ministry in Athens where Paul seemed to rely on his human intellect and philosophical arguments rather than the miracle ministry which characterized his evangelism in other venues.

However, the apostle does not place all the credit for the effectiveness of his ministry on signs and wonders alone. In I Thessalonians 1:5, Paul makes one simple statement that reveals five distinct elements in his approach to winning a city--five steps through the open door, if you wish to think of them as such.

> For our gospel came not unto you in word only, but also in power, and in the Holy Ghost, and in much assurance; as ye know what manner of men we were among you for your sake.

The first step he mentioned was the Word. Here he is talking about the gospel message which has been confirmed and proven through the scriptures and then presented within a biblical context. We must recognize that the good message is not always a sweet message; in fact, the scriptures teach that the gospel is definitely confrontational and possibly even offensive. It is called a stone of stumbling, a rock of offence, and a stone upon which we can fall and be broken or which will fall upon us and grind us to powder. (I Peter 2:8, Matthew 21:44, Luke 20:18) Paul described the situation in his day by saying that some preachers were filled with envy, strife, and contention as they preached; but God used them anyway. (Philippians 1:15-18)

Paul had a true desire to see people saved and he made a deliberate attempt to relate the gospel to them in a way that they would find relative and palatable. "To the weak became I as weak, that I might gain the weak: I am made all things to all men, that I might by all means save some." (I Corinthians 9:22) Like the Greeks with the Trojan horse and David at the watercourses of Jerusalem, the apostle looked for a way to get inside his target audience's defenses before he released his assault. In many cases, his subjects didn't even know what had hit them until they were fully in the grasp of the gospel. However, he was keenly aware that he could not influence them with anything short of the very Word of God. The scripture is full of instruction to avoid various substitutes which can camouflage themselves as worthy ministry material but actually lead to confusion and disqualification of our ministries: philosophy (Colossians 2:8), vain deceit (Colossians 2:8), the tradition of men (Colossians 2:8), the rudiments of the world (Colossians 2:8), enticing words of man's wisdom (I Corinthians 2:4), profane and vain babblings (I Timothy 6:20, II Timothy 2:16), oppositions of science falsely so called (I Timothy 6:20), fables (I Timothy 1:4, II Timothy 44), Jewish fables (Titus 1:14), profane and old wives' fables (I Timothy 4:7), cunningly devised fables (II Peter 1:16), endless genealogies (I Timothy 1:4, Titus 3:9), the commandments of men (Titus 1:14), foolish and unlearned questions (II Timothy 2:23, Titus 3:9), teachers having itching ears (II Timothy 4:3), teaching things which they ought not for filthy lucre's sake (Titus 1:11), strivings about the law (Titus 3:9), the commandments of men (Matthew 15:9, Mark 7:7, Colossians 2:22), the doctrines of men (Colossians 2:22), strange doctrines (Hebrews 13:9) and even doctrines of devils (I Timothy 4:1).

Paul's second step was power. All we need is a quick review of the book of Acts to see that his ministry was indeed accompanied with miraculous events. (Acts 13:11, 16:16-18, 19:11, 20:9-10, 28:3-6)

Next, Paul mentions the Holy Ghost. In that the operation of the gifts seems to have been his topic in the previous category, we must interpret this reference to suggest a fuller meaning of the operation of the Holy Spirit in the believer's life. Turning to his letter to the Galatians, we see at least two areas where the Holy Spirit's influence must be evidenced in a believer's life and ministry. The first is in chapter five verses sixteen and eighteen--walking in and being led by the Spirit. Such Holy Spirit orchestrated movement is not only vitally important to the success of our personal lives and the productivity of our ministries, but it may also make the difference between life and death. As Paul mentioned in the Galatian passage, the fatally destructive works of the flesh will overcome us unless we walk in the Spirit. The apostle was directed away from Asia toward a fertile ministry in Europe through the Holy Spirit's direction. The inner voice of the Holy Spirit also warned Paul of the impending danger into which his ship was to sail. (Acts 27:10) The other Holy Spirit quality that Paul discusses in Galatians chapter five is the fruit of the Spirit listed in verses twenty-two and twenty-three. Just as no one cares for a barren tree that does not produce fruit (Matthew 21:19, Luke 13:6-7), people will not be attracted to our lives or ministries unless we manifest the fruit of the Spirit.

Paul follows with the quality of assurance. Even without an examination of some of the key biblical injunctions concerning assurance (Isaiah 32:17, Acts 17:31, Colossians 2:2, Hebrews 6:11, and 10:22), we can recognize from the natural world that we never want to believe what someone is saying if we don't feel like he really believes it himself. I know that I'd never buy a car from a salesman if I saw him driving another make. Paul was persuaded of the validity of his message (Romans 8:38, 14:14, II Timothy 1:12) and admonished his disciples to be fully persuaded concerning their faith. (Romans 14:5)

Several years ago, a dear friend of mine was diagnosed as having an advanced case of one of the most aggressive kinds of cancer. In fact, when the doctor gave her the report, he advised her to go straight from his office to the airport and catch a plane to a special cancer clinic in Texas. He insisted that there was no time to delay--even to stop by her house and pack a suitcase for the trip. As believers, my friend and her husband determined that they would first have prayer before going for the specialized treatment. Their pastor called all the elders of the church together for a special prayer meeting and laid hands on my friend; however, she could sense doubt behind their prayer "of faith." She told her husband that she could hear what they were saying with their lips but could also read what they were thinking by looking at their eyes, faces, and body language -- and the two did not agree. She told him, "These people are not going to heal me; they are going to kill me! Please get me to a place where people really believe what they say!" When he promised to take her anywhere an airplane could fly, she asked to come to Indiana to be with my wife and me. I arranged for special prayer by two great apostles--our pastor, Dr. Lester Sumrall, and the pastor of the world's largest congregation, Dr. Yonggi Cho; then she spent the next three days in our home and received a constant diet of faith-filled words which came with confidence out of our hearts, not just words out of our heads. When she did check in at the cancer clinic, the doctor refused to admit her with the explanation that theirs was a specialized facility and only people with cancer could be treated there! For my friend -- and for each of us -- the treasure that is stored in the secret place of the heart was the difference between life and death. In Mark 11:23, Jesus emphasized that not doubting in the heart coupled with the positive confession is the key to a successful faith life. Paul also spoke of the power of coupling heart belief and the oral confession in Romans 10:10, while James 1:8 described the futility of having a heart and mouth which were not in agreement and Isaiah 29:13 concluded that such disagreement is abominable to God. The assurance we had in the Word of God was the key to saving this woman's life and it will be the key to saving the souls of those to whom we minister.

Character is the fifth step which Paul used to enter the city of Thessalonica with the gospel. In our Thessalonian passage, he called it his "manner of man." To get a definition of this term, we can turn to his farewell to the Ephesian church where again he used this same expression and gave a rather lengthy explanation. The purity of his motives and the unselfishness of his service permeate the speech and testify to the quality of life he lived before the people. Who he was backed up what he said. As the old expression goes, he walked the walk as well as talked the talk. Another couplet reminds us that people don't care how much you know unless they know how much you care. Our personal character is likely the most powerful force in communicating to the people we wish to win for Christ. After all, many more people will read our lives than will ever read our tracts.

> And when they were come to him, he said unto them, Ye know, from the first day that I came into Asia, after what manner I have been with you at all seasons, Serving the Lord with all humility of mind, and with many tears, and temptations, which befell me by the lying in wait of the Jews: And how I kept back nothing that was profitable unto you, but have shewed you, and have taught you publickly, and from house to house, testifying both to the Jews, and also to the Greeks, repentance toward God, and faith toward our Lord Jesus Christ...Wherefore I take you to record this day, that I am pure from the blood of all men. For I have not shunned to declare unto you all the counsel of God...Therefore watch, and remember, that by the space of three years I ceased not to warn every one night and day with tears...I have coveted no man's silver, or gold, or apparel. Yea, ye yourselves know, that these hands have ministered unto my necessities, and to them that were with me. (Acts 20:18-34)

We need not only develop a strategy for bringing in a harvest for Christ but also a strategy for keeping and preserving that harvest once we have gathered it. In other words, our evangelism must be followed with proper discipleship.

We can see an excellent example in the life of Paul--a man who was consumed with his love for the churches. Reading the introductions to his letters gives us a glimpse into his never-ending concern for the saints. To the Corinthians, he writes, "I thank my God <u>always</u> on your behalf." To the Philippians, he says, "I thank my God upon <u>every</u> remembrance of you." He addresses the Colossians, "We give thanks to God and the Father of our Lord Jesus Christ, praying <u>always</u> for you." His greeting to the Thessalonian church reads, "We give thanks to God <u>always</u> for you all, making mention of you in our prayers." He addresses Timothy as "my own son in the faith" and "my dearly beloved son" and goes on to say, "I thank God, whom I serve from my forefathers with pure conscience, that <u>without ceasing</u> I have remembrance of thee in my prayers night and day." Titus also receives the loving salutation of "mine own son after the common faith." In writing to Philemon, Paul also addresses Apphia whom he called "beloved" and then writes, "I thank my God, making mention of thee <u>always</u> in my prayers."

From these opening lines, we are able to get a glimpse inside the heart of a man who will be able to perpetuate change in a city. His converts were never out of his heart and mind. No matter how many miles and how many years separated them, these loved ones were always in Paul's prayers. But it is in his greeting to the church at Rome that we are able to really see what is in the heart of a true minister of God. Here Paul is addressing a church that he has never visited and a congregation of believers who, except for a few individuals, were strangers to him. Yet, he confirms--

and even calls upon God as his witness--that he is always and unceasingly interceding for them. This is a pastor's heart--a heart of unceasing love and concern for the Body of Christ, whether personal friends or total strangers. These believers he addresses as "beloved" and says,
> I thank my God through Jesus Christ for you all, that your faith is spoken of throughout the whole world. For God is my witness, whom I serve with my spirit in the gospel of his Son, that <u>without ceasing</u> I make mention of you <u>always</u> in my prayers.

In II Corinthians chapter eleven, Paul graphically illustrated how heavily the burden of love for the church weighed upon his heart. Here, he described the physical difficulties he endured for the gospel's sake: beatings, imprisonments, shipwrecks, long journeys, plots against his life, attacks of wild beasts, assaults by robbers, hunger, exposure, and being stoned to the point of death. Yet he concludes this list with, "Beside those things that are without, that which cometh upon me daily, the care of all the churches." (verse 28) He seems to be saying that the inner burden he carried for the churches exceeded the physical burdens that had been hurled upon him externally. He wrote lengthy and detailed letters to minister to them, he went to great lengthens to visit them and insure their well-being (Acts 15.36), and he sent others in his place to guarantee that they had proper instruction and solid leadership in place (Titus 1:5). This is the heart of a man who will see fruit that remains long after the initial revival.

But Paul is not our ultimate example; he was only outwardly manifesting the true life of Christ--the One who lived inside him. (Galatians 2:20) Luke 22:31

records that Jesus knew about Satan's plot to destroy Peter, so He prayed for him that he would not fall. In Matthew 23:37, we read that Jesus sat on the Mount of Olives and overlooked the city of Jerusalem with a heart that cried out for its people. He wanted to call them under His wings of protection but they would not come to Him. It broke His heart because His was a true shepherd's heart. The gospels continually repeat the theme that Jesus was moved with compassion for the people--the key to others' hearts and lives. When Jesus tried to illustrate what was in His heart, He used parables of a shepherd and his sheep. In Luke 15:4-7, He demonstrated that a shepherd is never satisfied until he has done everything possible to rescue every possible sheep.

> What man of you, having an hundred sheep, if he lose one of them doth not leave the ninety and nine in the wilderness, and go after that which is lost, until he find it? And when he hath found it, he layeth it on his shoulders, rejoicing. And when he cometh home, he calleth together his friends and neighbors, saying unto them, Rejoice with me; for I have found my sheep which was lost. I say unto you, that likewise joy shall be in heaven over one sinner that repenteth, more than over ninety and nine just persons, which need no repentance.

The parable of the Good Shepherd in John 10:1-16, of course, speaks of Christ's love for the church, but it also illustrates the kind of heart that must be in any true minister through whom Christ's life is to be manifest.

Verily, verily, I say unto you, He that entereth not by the door into the sheepfold but climbeth up some other way, the same is a thief and a robber. But he that entereth in by the door is the shepherd of the sheep. To him the porter openeth; and the sheep hear his voice: and he calleth his own sheep by name, and leadeth them out. And when he putteth forth his own sheep, he goeth before them, and the sheep follow him: for they know his voice. And a stranger will they not follow, but will flee from him: for they know not the voice of strangers. This parable spake Jesus unto them: but they understood not what things they were which he spake unto them. Then said Jesus unto them again, Verily, verily, I say unto you, I am the door of the sheep. All that ever came before me are thieves and robbers: but the sheep did not hear them. I am the door: by me if any man enter in, he shall be saved, and shall go in and out, and find pasture. The thief cometh not, but for to steal, and to kill and to destroy: I am come that they might have life, and that they might have it more abundantly. I am the good shepherd: the good shepherd giveth his life for the sheep. But he that is an hireling fleeth, because he is an hireling, and careth not for the sheep. I am the good shepherd, and know my sheep, and am known of mine. As the Father knoweth me, even so know I the Father: and I lay down my life for the sheep. And other sheep I have, which are not of this fold: them also I must bring, and they shall hear my voice; and there shall be one fold, and one shepherd.

In John 21:15-17, the resurrected Lord confronted Simon Peter with the challenge that if he truly loved the Master, he would become a shepherd of the flock and "feed the sheep." Peter apparently learned his lesson well and challenged others who wanted to become ministers in the Body of Christ to develop a shepherd's heart.

The elders which are among you I exhort, who am also an elder, and a witness of the sufferings of Christ, and also a partaker of the glory that shall be revealed: Feed the flock of God which is among you, taking the oversight thereof, not by constraint, but willingly; nor for filthy lucre, but of a ready mind; Neither as being lords over God's heritage, but being examples to the flock. And when the chief Shepherd shall appear, ye shall receive a crown of glory that fadeth not away. Likewise, ye younger, submit yourselves unto the elder. Yea, all of you be subject one to another, and be clothed with humility: for God resisteth the proud, and giveth grace to the humble. (I Peter 5:1-5)

In the words of both Jesus and Peter, a shepherd

is not someone who has the position for a paycheck. It has been my experience that those men and women who are really called into the ministry and have a desire to win their cities for Christ would almost be willing to pay to get to do their work. To them, their positions are ministries, not jobs.

However, not all ministers have this pure heart of a true shepherd. Listen to how the prophet Jeremiah described some of the ministers of his day--and of our day, as well,

> Woe be unto the pastors that destroy and scatter the sheep of my pasture! saith the LORD. Therefore thus saith the LORD God of Israel against the pastors that feed my people; Ye have scattered my flock, and driven them away, and have not visited them: behold, I will visit upon you the evil of your doings, saith the LORD. And I will gather the remnant of my flock out of all countries whither I have driven them, and will bring them again to their folds; and they shall be fruitful and increase. And I will set up shepherds over them which shall feed them: and they shall fear no more, nor be dismayed, neither shall they be lacking, saith the LORD. (verses 23:1-4)

In this remarkable passage, God demonstrates His personal desire to see that the flock is shepherded. The story of Jonah's evangelism in the Assyrian capital of Nineveh is marked by the unwillingness of the prophet to minister to the people and his utter dismay at the fact that God actually forgave these pagans.

(Jonah 4:1, 2, 10, 11) Unlike the disgruntled prophet who wanted to draw a small circle and leave certain individuals and entire ethnic groups outside, our God draws a huge circle that includes everyone. Second Peter 3:9 described the heart of our heavenly Father this way, "The Lord is not slack concerning his promise, as some men count slackness; but is longsuffering to us-ward, not willing that any should perish, but that all should come to repentance." From the first page of your Bible to its closing paragraphs, He is portrayed as an all-inclusive God. At least four times the Lord reiterates that He intended to bless the entire human family through the descendents of His servant Abraham. (Genesis 18:18, 22:18, 26:4, Galatians 3:8) The Psalmist crafted a poetic prophecy affirming the all-inclusive nature of the Lord's love, "All the ends of the world shall remember and turn unto the LORD: and all the kindreds of the nations shall worship before thee." (verse 22:27) The same sentiment was heralded by Isaiah at least twice during his prophetic ministry, "And it shall come to pass in the last days, that the mountain of the LORD'S house shall be established in the top of the mountains, and shall be exalted above the hills; and all nations shall flow unto it…This is the purpose that is purposed upon the whole earth: and this is the hand that is stretched out upon all the nations." (verses 2:2, 14:26) Two different prophets proclaim that the entire earth will be inundated with the glory of the Lord. (Isaiah 11:9, Habakkuk 2:14) The Old Testament declares and the New Testament confirms that it is the Lord's intent to pour out His Spirit on all flesh. (Joel 2:28, Acts 2:17) Jesus personally took His ministry to every city and then commissioned His followers to do likewise. (Luke 8:1-4, 10:1) He left no question in the minds of His followers that He intended that no one be excluded from receiving His message. (Matthew 24:14, 28:19, Mark 13:10, 16:15, Luke 24:47) The Apocalypse concludes with a futuristic insight into the time when this all-inclusive work will be accomplished. (verses 7:9, 11:15, 21:24)

Because the Philadelphian church had the key of David of a pure heart and used it to go through the open door to bring the good news of the gospel into their world, the Lord promised to preserve them from the coming hour of temptation. We can expect the same preservation if we will follow their pattern of heeding the Word of God.

Laodicea--Perplexity of Perception

In the letter to the church at Laodicea (Revelation 3:14-22), the Risen Lord deals with the perplexity of perception--men who don't know who they really are. These church members perceived themselves as rich when they were actually wretched, poor, miserable, naked, and blind. The Lord used the irony of the city's water system to expose the folly within the church. Because the city was located a few miles from a hot spring on one side and an ice-cold spring on the other side, the city engineers had developed a plan to pipe in both hot and cold water to supply their residents. The only problem was that they didn't calculate that the hot water would cool down in transit and that the sun would heat up the cold water as it traveled to the city. Instead of hot and cold water, they wound up with both systems delivering lukewarm water! Relying upon their own human resources, resourcefulness, and intelligence, the leaders in the church at Laodicea thought they were delivering something worthwhile to their congregation and city. All the while, Jesus was standing outside knocking, asking to be re-invited into the church so that

He could give them new life and meaning. His promise to those who would repent and be renewed is that they would be invited to sit with Him in His throne with the Father. In all actuality, this provision to sit with Christ in heavenly places with authority over all principalities, powers, and dominions is available to all believers according to Ephesians 2:6 and 1:20. Unfortunately, most of us do not perceive ourselves as having attained--or ever being able to attain--that position. Again, our problem is the same as that of the Laodiceans, only in reverse.

I hope that no one who is involved with any twelve-step recovery program will be offended by this analogy, but we must learn not to have what I call the "Alcoholics Anonymous" mentality. I use this term because the approach used in this sort of addiction and dependency recovery program is to keep the individual constantly aware of his potential of falling back into the trap from which he has been freed. Individuals within this kind of program are taught to say that they are alcoholics even though they may have been sober for thirty years. There is certainly some merit in such a mentality in that it helps the subjects avoid compromising situations which could hurl them back into the snare of their addictions. The problem with this mindset is that it fails to allow the individual to see himself the way God sees him--as a new creature in Christ whose old man has passed away and in whom all things have become new. (II Corinthians 5:17) Let's look at just a few biblical examples and see how this "Alcoholics Anonymous" mentality tried to sabotage their destinies.

Gideon had this mental attitude concerning his family background. In Judges 6:11, we read his evaluation of his heritage, "Oh my Lord, wherewith shall

I save Israel? Behold, my family is poor in Manasseh, and I am the least in my father's house." Until Gideon was able to renew his thinking to come into alignment with how God saw him--as a mighty man of valor--he was bound by the fact that he didn't come from the right family stock. Had Gideon not been able to change his thoughts about himself, his opinion of himself as having come from the "wrong side of the tracks" would have short-circuited his future and the mighty work he was called to do.

When God called Jeremiah, he responded that he couldn't do anything significant because he was too young, "Then said I, Ah, Lord God! Behold, I cannot speak: for I am a child." (Jeremiah 1:6) While Jeremiah was looking at his youth and seeing it as a disqualifier, God was looking at his youthfulness as the ticket to a long and profitable ministry. To God, the younger the prophet could start, the better; that meant that there would be that many more years for him to minister. Had the prophet not broken out of the "Alcoholics Anonymous" mentality, he would have wasted the best years of his life--and maybe his entire life. For certain, he would have missed the most significant of his appointments with destiny.

Isaiah had an "Alcoholics Anonymous" mentality about his spirituality--or lack thereof. When the Lord appeared to him and called him into the ministry, he tried to back out of the picture, citing his sinfulness "Woe is me! For I am undone; because I am a man of unclean lips, and I dwell in the midst of a people of unclean lips: for mine eyes have seen the King, the Lord of hosts." (Isaiah 6:5) We have no idea what kind of language Isaiah might have been using up to this point, but his encounter with the thrice-holy God made him uncomfortably aware of how damnable it really was. Had God not sent an angel to touch his lips with a coal from the altar, the prophet would never have begun to see himself as acceptable before such a radically holy God--and he, therefore, would have been cheated out of the privilege of serving as one of God's most outstanding spokesmen.

Even Moses was enslaved by this "Alcoholics Anonymous" mentality in regard to his natural abilities. When arrested by the call of God issuing from a burning bush, he argued back, "O my Lord, I am not eloquent, neither heretofore, nor since thou hast spoken unto thy servant: but I am slow of speech, and of a slow tongue." (Exodus 4:10) It was only after God began to perform miracles through him that Moses learned that when you can turn sticks into snakes, it doesn't matter if you stutter.

Ten of the spies whom Moses sent to spy out the Promised Land had poor self-images when they compared themselves to their enemies. Though God saw them as leaders and princes among their tribes, these spies saw themselves as grasshoppers. As a result, they became as grasshoppers before the sons of Anak. "And there we saw the giants, the sons of Anak, which come of the giants: and we were in our own sight as grasshoppers, and so we were in their sight." (Numbers 13:33)

The prodigal son came back to the father's house but was afraid to accept the father's grace because he had a poor image of himself and could not see himself as worthy of being forgiven and accepted. Even though he overcame his "Alcoholics Anonymous" mentality enough to come home, that "stinking thinking" tried to continue to keep him in slavery even in the father's house. (Luke 15:19) Tragically, we all too often mirror this same fate when, even after coming to Christ for salvation, we fail to get the full revelation of exactly who God is and wants to be in our lives. When the prodigal son's father gave him a grand reception and established him in a place of honor, it was not so much a statement of the son's worthiness but a demonstration of the graciousness of the father. In our lives, God wants to manifest His goodness to and through us because He wants us to be established as testimonies to His goodness and demonstrations of His blessing. (Deuteronomy 7:6)

We must not look back at our origins and our past. God is not interested in where we are coming from, but where we are going to. In Jeremiah 29:11, the Lord affirms that He is interested in bringing us to an expected end with an established future--regardless of where we began or how shaky our past might have been.

In order to overcome the "Alcoholics Anonymous" mentality, we must develop the II Corinthians 5:17 mentality that proclaims that we are new creatures in Christ and that old things are passed away while all things are now new. We must also cultivate the Romans 8:37 mentality which declares that we more than conquerors through Christ. We must counter the "Alcoholics Anonymous" mentality with the Philippians 4:13 mindset that boasts that we can do all things through Christ. We can teardown the stronghold of the "Alcoholics Anonymous" mentality by renewing our minds to the realities of Romans 5:10 through confessing that God will do anything for us now that we are His sons because He loved us enough to die for us even while we were still His enemies. We must openly confront the negativism of the "Alcoholics Anonymous" mentality by clinging tenaciously to the John 14:12 mentality that declares that we can do even greater works than Jesus did.

When asked what it means to be more than a conqueror, one Bible teacher explained it with the analogy of a prize fighter and his wife. The boxer went into the ring with a vicious antagonist. After suffering blows, lacerations, contusions, and bruises, he finally landed the winning punch which sent his opponent to the mat. He then crawled out of the ring as the champion--a conqueror--and was handed a sizable check for having won the bout. As soon as he arrived at home, his wife happily took the check and started spending it. She did not have to go into the ring and take any blows or lose any blood, but she got the cash--she was more than a conqueror. In the spirit realm, we are just like that wife; we get all the rewards even though it was Christ who faced the enemy and defeated him at the cross. We do not have to do the battling--in fact, we couldn't even if it was up to us to do so. We must learn, as did Jehoshaphat, to stand still and see the salvation of the Lord. (II Chronicles 20:17) No matter how much we think that we might be able to accomplish with our travailing intercession, languishing fasts, or vehement spiritual warring, we must be cautious to not go back to a "conqueror mentality" when we are called to have a "more than conqueror mentality."

One side note of caution must be added here: at the same time that we are learning not to think too lowly of ourselves, we have to be careful not to join the Laodiceans and get too cocky and begin to think more highly of ourselves than we ought to think. (Romans 12:3) Judas though too much of himself and believed that he could handle gold without letting it take hold of him. Wrong! (John 12:6) Samson thought that he could play with the girls without getting into trouble.

Wrong, again! (Judges 14:3) Nadab and Abihu found that trying to take God's glory was like playing with fire which cannot be done without getting burned. (Leviticus 10:1-2)

We must constantly live our lives in the tension between striving to make sure that we don't fail to take advantage of all that Jesus has provided for us (Hebrews 4:11) and thinking that we can do it ourselves. For the Laodiceans, the problem was having too high a perception of themselves; for most of us, the problem is having too low a perception of ourselves. In either case, the solution is the same: take the key of David, a pure heart before the Lord, and walk boldly through the open door He sets before us. However, the one prerequisite is that we also use that key to open a door for Him to enter our lives and take His rightful place on the throne of our hearts.

Having Ears to Hear

As we took our theological tour through the churches of Asia Minor, we were confronted with a multitude of different spiritual conditions: the predicament of passion, the presence of persecution, the pitfalls of permissiveness, the problem of perversion, probing perfection, the purity of purpose, and the perplexity of perception. Certainly, we found that one or more of the issues confronting these believers are just as real in our present lives as they were in the days of John's incarceration on the Isle of Patmos. It is exactly because of the universality of these problems that each letter contains the injunction, "He that hath an ear let him hear what the Spirit saith unto the churches." Notice that in each statement the mandate is to hear not only what is said to the individual church being addressed but to hear what the

Spirit is saying to all the churches collectively. To properly become into the church God desires us to be, we must adequately deal with each of these multi-faceted aspects of the faith and allow the Holy Spirit to speak directly into our lives in each of these dimensions.

Although it is only necessary for God to say something one time for it to be an unequivocal truth, the Lord so wanted to unquestionably confirm these mandates in our lives that He addressed the same concepts during His incarnate ministry as well as during this post-resurrection visitation with John the Revelator. In Mark 8:18 in the context of the feeding of the four thousand, Jesus asked, "Don't you have ears?"--addressing the same issue which He brought before the church at Ephesus: "Are you too busy working for Me that you can't hear Me as I speak and minister to you?" In Matthew 11:15, He again commanded that those who have ears should hear. This time, it was in context of His teaching concerning the fact that the kingdom of God will suffer violence--the same message addressed in the letter to the church at Smyrna. The parable of the tares contains the quote about having ears to hear (Matthew 13:43) when Jesus explained that there will be counterfeits scattered among the true believers--the same problem of permissiveness which faced the church at Pergamos. The phrase appears again in Mark 7:16 when Jesus speaks of things that can defile--the same problem He addressed in the message to the church at Thyatira. We find the phrase in Mark 4:23 when Jesus says that nothing will be hidden--a vital element in probing perfection as in the message to the church at Sardis. Each time the parable of the four soils (also know as the parable of the sower) appears in the scriptures, the mandate that those with ears must hear is again quoted (Mark 4:9, Matthew 13:9, Luke 8:8). This parable's emphasis on the increase in the harvest carries the same message we see in the open door which is set before the church at Philadelphia. One last appearance of this phrase occurs in Luke 14:35 when Jesus talks about flavorless salt--a direct parallel to the condition seen in the church at Laodicea.

As one pastor said when I spoke at his church and ministered on the same passages he had been preaching on even though I did not know about his previous sermons, "God is speaking in stereo. We'd better listen!" If we have ears, let's hear what He is saying to all the churches. If these messages had to be given to the churches before Jesus could reveal anything to them concerning the last days, how much more must we understand them since we are actually living in the end times.

Seeking the Glory of the Nations

One of the promises of the end time is that the glory of the Lord will be revealed throughout the earth (Habakkuk 2:14) and that the glory of the nations will be given over to the kingdom of God (Revelation 21:24, 26). Revelation 7:9 and 15:4 depict a time when people of every nation, kindred, people, and tongue will stand before the throne of God and worship Him. Revelation 11:15 further confirms that every nation will eventually become part of the divine kingdom. Twice in chapter twenty-one, the prophet predicts that the rulers of the nations will bring their glory and honor into the kingdom of God. (verses 24, 26)

With this truth in mind, we must take a new look at the world around us, trying to understand how every kingdom can contribute to God's ultimate plan and be part of the glorious finale of history.

The Taj Mahal! Beautiful white marble, perfectly symmetrical with a sparkling white dome amid four elegant minarets, it is considered to be the most beautiful building in the world. Standing before it was truly a breath-taking experience. I wandered through its great chambers, across its great plazas, around its stunning gardens, and beside its beautiful reflection pools for hours. I was totally enthralled by the magnificence of the splendid structure. I marveled at the exquisite inlaid stonework. As a mausoleum to his favorite wife, the Taj was a tomb fit for a queen and only affordable by a great Indian maharajah. This was the glory and grandeur of Mother India.

After India, my Asian odyssey took me to Sri Lanka, the ancient Ceylon. There, I had the wonderful experience of witnessing the Parahara, an annual festival celebrating Buddha's tooth which is preserved in the great temple in Kandy. Inside five coffins of gold and silver rests the sacred remain of Siddhartha Gautama, the Buddha. Once each year, this hallowed molar is brought from the temple and paraded through the streets of the mountain capital of this resplendent island nation. Nine days of festivities lead up to the climatic moment when the most sacred object of the Buddhist faith begins its journey through the city. Thousands of celebrants had gathered to witness the parade of more than one hundred and fifty decorated elephants, hundreds of native dancers, jugglers, acrobats, and marching bands as they escorted the massive male elephant which bore the revered relic. Words cannot describe the excitement that rushed through my being as I stood in the press of the crowd watching the seemingly endless parade of elephants and dancers preceding the awesome tusker decorated with tiny glowing light bulbs and the golden coffin.

Having completed my ministry in the Indian subcontinent, I moved on to the Land of the Rising Sun--Japan. Traveling through the islands, I had occasions to visit many of the elegant temples and shrines of the land. Kyoto and Nara were ancient capitals with some of the most beautifully preserved shrines and gardens. Here, I found the kind of serene beauty that only the Japanese can model. Long, quiet, meditative strolls through the deer parks, beside the garden pools, and around the ancient temples gave birth to unsurpassed calm and contemplation. Again in Japan, I found beauty and grandeur. It was unlike that of India or Ceylon, but it is a treasured experience.

These experiences of the magnificence of nations and cultures rushed through my very soul as I read a biblical passage about the glory of heaven. John the Revelator, using the imagery of the ancient practice of subservient nations paying royal tribute to the king of the dominate nations, wrote,

> And the nations of them which are saved shall walk in the light of it: and the kings of the earth do bring their glory and honor into it. And the gates of it shall not be shut at all by day: for there shall be no night there. And they shall bring the glory and honor of the nations into it. (Revelation 21:24-26)

In my mind, I could see Indira Ghandhi, who was still alive and the uncontested Prime Minister of India at that time, arrayed in an exquisite Indian sari, bowing low before the throne of the Almighty to present to Him the glory and honor of the Taj Mahal as a tribute. Following Miss Ghandhi came then-president Jayewardene of Sri Lanka prostrating himself before the Ancient of Days to humbly offer the Parahara as a tribute for the kingdom of God. Next came Hirohito, who had not yet passed away and stood as supreme emperor of Japan. In traditional Japanese fashion of courtesy and humility, he bowed time and time again, lower and lower each time to indicate reverence for Him Who Sat Upon the Throne. Finally--as he had bent himself as deeply as possible--with fear that his gift was not good enough, he presented the glory and grandeur of Kyoto and Nara to God.

The kings of the nations were bringing the glory and honor of the earth into the city of God. Or were they? Almost as quickly as my mind had conjured the image of this oriental parade into the New Jerusalem, my spirit brought it to a screeching halt as the Holy Spirit directed me back to the passage. This time my attention was drawn to a little phrase that I had previously overlooked: "them which are saved." I was also drawn to one further verse, "And there shall in no wise enter into it anything that defileth, neither maketh a lie: but they which are written in the Lamb's book of life." (verse 21:27)

Now, my mind was drawn to another of my experiences in Japan. It was a quiet afternoon I had spent with an elderly Japanese pastor and his wife as they shared with me their testimonies. During World War II, since Japan and the US were enemies, all Japanese Christians were considered to be traitors because the nationalist government saw them as members of an American religion. This dear pastor had been arrested and condemned to spend the four years between Pearl Harbor and Hiroshima in a four-foot-by-four-foot oriental prison cael. Even though the wife was not incarcerated, she was placed under house arrest and subjected to daily interrogation. This precious couple endured innumerable beatings and indescribable persecutions, yet they never flinched in the face of opposition. Their unwavering faith was a crown of life that shone almost visibly as they shared their stories. "This," the Holy Spirit said, "is the glory and honor of the nation." Then the Lord asked me, "To whom is the Taj Mahal dedicated?" "Mohammed," was my answer. Next the Lord questioned me about the Parahara, and I answered, "To Buddha." Finally, His query turned to Nara and Kyoto and responded that they were dedicated to the Shinto kami. Yet, the little Japanese pastor and his wife were dedicated totally to Jesus. This is the glory and honor of a nation.

Years later, this whole vision came pouring back into my spirit as I visited the former Russian provincial capital of Leningrad. Formerly the great St. Petersburg which boasted, and rightfully so, to be Europe's northern Paris, Leningrad is resplendent with cathedrals, palaces, and art treasures that rival any other throughout the world. It was more than I could comprehend as I walked through palace after palace with massive walls covered with elegant golden facade. Room after room was filled with furniture of pure gold. Fabulous cathedrals sported golden domes. Museums held unbelievable collections of masterpieces including Van Goghs, Rembrandts, and Picassos. I felt as if my eyes would pop out of my head as I moved from one breath-taking scene to the next. Yet it was not in the palaces, museums, or cathedrals that I found the real treasures of the Soviet Union. It was in a humble three-room apartment where a handful of believers gathered that I witnessed the glory and honor of the USSR. Believers, who had been subjected to years of communism's insistence that there is no God, knew that He did exist for His presence permeated their little gathering. This was the exaltation of the nation. "Righteousness exalteth a nation: but sin is a reproach to any people." (Proverbs 14:34) In a nation dedicated to humanism and man's accomplishments without even acknowledging God's existence, this handful of believers was a repository of glory and honor that was probably noticed only by the Lord Himself.

When I stopped to consider that the glory and honor which was to be brought into the New Jerusalem was to enhance and add to the glory already existing in the city, I realized how foolish it was to even think that the gold-plated furnishings of Leningrad could embellish a city whose streets are of such exquisitely pure gold that it becomes transparent. How preposterous it is to even imagine that the polished marble of the Taj Mahal would add to, rather than distract from, the grandeur of a city whose foundations and walls are made of such fabulous gem stones that the ordinary man finds it difficult to even pronounce their name, much less image their splendor.

But before we discuss how anyone will ever be able to add to the grandeur of that heavenly city, let's consider the one word that arrested my attention when I read this chapter--"saved." I suppose that this term is a bit out of vogue these days. We generally substitute words like "become a believer," "accept Christ," "become a Christian," or "be born again." While all these are powerful terms which convey the impact of conversion, perhaps the expression "saved" leaves us a bit unsure as to what we are actually trying to communicate. If a man is drowning, we instantly understand that he needs to be saved from the waters which threaten his life. If a lady is being attacked by a rapist, we have no problem recognizing that she must be saved from her attacker. Unfortunately we seem to be almost unaware that we live in a spiritual environment which is equally as threatening as that crazed sexual predator ready to molest the defenseless woman or the raging sea ready to engulf a man overboard. The Bible makes it unquestionably clear that there are malevolent forces at work in our world which will destroy any and every victim they can capture. The devil and the demonic fallen angels who assist him have an agenda which includes the total devastation of every area of the lives of their victims-- body, soul, and spirit. Just as the fourth man appeared in Nebuchadnezzar's fiery furnace to rescue Shadrach, Meshach, and Abednego--our God has a plan to step into the lives of all who will allow Him in to rescue them not only from the destruction of the furnace but also from even being tainted by the smell of its smoke. This kind of all-inclusive rescue and preservation is what God desired to communicate when He dictated the word "saved" into the hearts of the men who penned the words of the Bible.

Although the term may not be the most popular and it may not be considered the most politically correct wording today, I remember a day when "saved" was the common term people used to describe their regeneration. Although I could never prove it scientifically or with any statistical studies, it seems to me that along with the decline in the use of this archaic term there also came a corresponding decline in a lifestyle within the church which was free from the lingering scents and reeking odors of worldliness within the church.

As a child, I grew up among simple folk in a little church in a cotton mill town in South Carolina. Every Wednesday evening and occasionally on Sunday evening, we would have testimony services. One by one, the members of the congregation would stand to their feet and testify, "I'm saved, sanctified, filled with heaven's sweet Holy Ghost, added to the great Church of God, and on my way to heaven. Ya'll pray for me that I'll ever stand true." If there were fifty people present, forty-nine of them would stand up and testify, "I'm saved, sanctified, filled with heaven's sweet Holy Ghost, added to the great Church of God, and on my way to heaven. Ya'll pray for me that I'll ever stand true." Finally, the fiftieth person--most often a little old lady, sometimes a middle-aged gentleman, occasionally a younger person--would rise, sobbing into a handkerchief, and between the tears would stammer out, "I wasn't going to say nothing tonight. I told myself that I was just gonna set here. But I can't stand to fail to testify for my Lord. It's like fire shut up in my bones. I've just got to testify for my Jesus. I'm saved, sanctified, filled with heaven's sweet Holy Ghost, added to the great Church of God, and on my way to heaven. Ya'll pray for me that I'll ever stand true."

Over the years, I've gotten a lot of laughs out of the memories of those old testimony meetings; but as I've matured, I've come to understand that--although the words had become little more than a religious formula--they were once a vital testimony which rather fully expressed the reality of what it means to be saved. When I think of the first affirmation in the cliché which declares that the individual is saved, I call to memory a statement by one of my aunts who did not come to Christ as her personal savior until late in her adult life. Though she attended church regularly, she lived a rather carnal life and readily acknowledged that she was not saved. When challenged with her need for salvation, she would answer that she would someday get saved but that she was going to get saved the way they did at "Johnny's church"--referring to my dad's church where the people were all saved, sanctified, filled with heaven's sweet Holy Ghost, on their way to heaven, and asking that everyone would pray for them to ever stand true. She said that because she had seen dramatic transformations in people like our town drunk and so many others who had been considered lost causes until they got saved in our church. When she did finally get saved, my aunt wept bitterly at the altar until her life was truly and radically altered by God. She had been genuinely saved; she had not just made a simple profession of faith or joined the church.

The next description, "sanctified," means to be separated or set apart. When I hear this term I think of the money in my wallet because I have a divided compartment where I always keep a little cash which I don't intend to spend except in case of a real emergency. That cash is sanctified or set apart from normal purposes for a very special use under only specific situations. I keep it in a secret compartment so that it is out of normal sight when the wallet is opened because I want to avoid the temptation to use the money for general purposes. Our God does exactly the same thing with those who will allow it. The ninety-first Psalms speaks of a secret place where believers can dwell under the wings of the Almighty to find a special protection from the attacks of the enemy who would desire to destroy their lives--body, soul, and spirit. Those who allow themselves to be brought into this secret place of sanctification are genuinely saved from the destruction which could otherwise befall them.

To be filled with heaven's sweet Holy Ghost is one of the most powerful forces which a Christian can invoke in his life. In fact, Jesus warned His disciples that this was to be the first priority in their lives after He left them to return to the Father. He commanded that they should not do anything or go anywhere until they had received this divine indwelling. There are many benefits from being filled with the Holy Spirit, but let me focus on just one aspect--the empowering to live the sanctified life characteristic of a truly saved person. (II Thessalonians 2:13)

David Wilkerson, in his groundbreaking testimonial The Cross and the Switchblade, told the story of how he had naively followed the prompting of the Lord to go into the gangland of New York City to rescue the lives of the young men trapped in addictions and snares of devil. When this little Pentecostal preacher from the quiet countryside of Pennsylvania found himself dealing with the violent and hardened gang lords in the ghettos of the big city, he realized that there was only one thing that would ensure that the young men and women he was able to reach could ever stay free from the forces which had so solidly bound them before. He knew that they would have to not only be born again, they needed to also be filled with the Holy Spirit. His little book recorded that individuals who followed the Lord into this Holy Spirit encounter were the ones who also overcame their drug addictions and other bondages.

I once prayed with a young woman who had turned to the bottle during a time of stress in her life. Eventually, she realized that alcohol was controlling her life. As we prayed for deliverance from its addictive power, I was prompted to quote Ephesians 5:18 to her. When I instructed her to be filled with the Spirit rather than to be drunk with wine, she burst forth in a heavenly language. As soon as she began to speak in tongues, a foul smell of alcohol filled the area--an apparent manifestation of the demon of alcohol as it left her.

Of course, when the good folk in my little mill-hill church boasted of having been added to the great Church of God, they were making the distinction that they were members of that particular denomination as opposed to being Baptists or Methodists; however, the power of the statement is that they were actually members of the universal church of God consisting of all saved men and women--including the Baptists and Methodists. Being part of the church makes us all members of the Body of Christ and members one of another. That way we each are able to add to the whole our own unique giftings. (I Corinthians 12:7-12, Ephesians 4:16) The necessity of being part of the total Body of Christ is so significant that the author of Hebrews left us with a direct command that we should not forsake gathering together as a body of believers, and especially so in light of the fact that trying times are approaching. (verse 10:25)

    The next phase in the testimonial was "on my way to heaven," an affirmation of the believer's eternal focus. To see the power of having our focus on heaven, let's take a quick look at the life of the Apostle Paul. We have already quoted the comprehensive description he gave in II Corinthians of what it had cost him to be a Christian: abundant labors, stripes above measure, frequent imprisonments, often being in danger of death, five occasions when the Jews beat him with thirty-nine stripes, three occasions when he was beaten with rods, being stoned until he appeared to be dead, three shipwrecks, being afloat in the ocean for a full night and day, uncalculated traveling, perils of waters, perils of robbers, perils of his own countrymen, perils by the heathen, perils in the city, perils in the wilderness, perils in the sea, perils among false brethren, weariness, painfulness, constantly being on guard for those who are threatening him, hunger, thirst, frequent fasting, not having adequate clothing against the cold, and constant concern for the churches which he cared for. (verses 11:23-28) Yet listen to how he sums up all these experiences: "Our light affliction, which is but for a moment, worketh for us a far more exceeding and eternal weight of glory." (verse 4:17) In other words, he had his eyes so focused on the heaven he was going to that he hardly noticed the hell he was going through. It is this kind of determination to press for the mark (Philippians 3:14, Hebrews 12:1-2) that makes us able to have the staying power which is necessary to endure to the end--the quality necessary to truly be saved and qualify as one of the nations which can bring glory and honor into the New Jerusalem! (Matthew 24:13, Mark 13:13)

    Finally, the saints would always invoke the

prayers of the other saints so they would be able to ever stand true. It is vitally important that we recognize the need for the support of other members in the Body of Christ. The Bible is full of examples of prayers for members within the community of faith. We could fill pages with biblical quotes showing the significance, power, and necessity of praying for one another. However, I will only cite one verse in illustrating this point. There is one little detail we should pay attention to in I Timothy 2:1 as Paul admonished Timothy in his intercessory prayer life. "I exhort therefore, that, first of all, supplications, prayers, intercessions, and giving of thanks, be made for all men." Did you notice that he instructs Timothy that prayer should be his first directive? He assigns his young protégé the seemingly overwhelming task of establishing proper order in the church, but instructs him that the first step is prayer, the same pattern we will discover in Paul's own ministry if we simply read through the introductory paragraphs of his epistles.

Before we go any further in our discussion of salvation, I'd like to make one interesting observation about why we are saved. Our salvation is for God's own purposes--not simply to keep us out of hell! (Psalms 106:8) Notice what Paul says in II Timothy 1:9, "Who hath saved us, and called us with an holy calling, not according to our works, but according to his own purpose and grace, which was given us in Christ Jesus before the world began." God has a purpose in saving humans; He wants to mold us into masterpieces of His grace. As Michelangelo had his statue of David and the Sistine Chapel, God has regenerated humans as His show pieces.

Ephesians 1:3-12 explains that God's whole plan in saving man is so that he will be able to manifest honor and bring praise to the glory of God through his redemption and regenerated personality:

> Blessed be the God and Father of our Lord Jesus Christ, who hath blessed us with all spiritual blessings in heavenly places in Christ: According as he hath chosen us in him before the foundation of the world, that we should be holy and without blame before him in love: Having predestinated us unto the adoption of children by Jesus Christ to himself, according to the good pleasure of his will, To the praise of the glory of his grace, wherein he hath made us accepted in the beloved. In whom we have redemption through his blood, the forgiveness of sins, according to the riches of his grace; Wherein he hath abounded toward us in all wisdom and prudence; Having made known unto us the mystery of his will, according to his good pleasure which he hath purposed in himself: That in the dispensation of the fulness of times he might gather together in one all things in Christ, both which are in heaven, and which are on earth; even in him: In whom also we have obtained an inheritance, being predestinated according to the purpose of him who worketh all things after the counsel of his own will: That we should be to the praise of his glory, who first trusted in Christ.

Possibly the best loved passages of the two

testaments proclaim the same truth. In the Old Testament, the twenty-third Psalm tells us that the Good Shepherd leads His sheep in the paths of righteousness for His name's. It is not so much for the benefit of the sheep as it is for the purpose of bringing honor and creditability to the name of the Shepherd. In the New Testament, the Lord's Prayer begins with the imperative "Hallowed be thy name." This clause could also be read, "Let Your name be honored," implying, "Let me be a good example for You," or "Let me reflect you." The principle is more explicitly spelled out elsewhere in the Sermon on the Mount when Jesus said, "Let your light so shine before men, that they may see your good works, and glorify your Father which is in heaven." (Matthew 5:16)

Isaiah 45:17-23 gives us a number of powerful insights into God's plan of salvation:

> But Israel shall be saved in the LORD with an everlasting salvation: ye shall not be ashamed nor confounded world without end. For thus saith the LORD that created the heavens; God himself that formed the earth and made it; he hath established it, he created it not in vain, he formed it to be inhabited: I am the LORD; and there is none else. I have not spoken in secret, in a dark place of the earth: I said not unto the seed of Jacob, Seek ye me in vain: I the LORD speak righteousness, I declare things that are right. Assemble yourselves and come; draw near together, ye that are escaped of the nations: they have no knowledge that set up the wood of their graven image,

> and pray unto a god that cannot save. Tell ye, and bring them near; yea, let them take counsel together: who hath declared this from ancient time? who hath told it from that time? have not I the LORD? and there is no God else beside me; a just God and a Saviour; there is none beside me. Look unto me, and be ye saved, all the ends of the earth: for I am God, and there is none else. I have sworn by myself, the word is gone out of my mouth in righteousness, and shall not return, That unto me every knee shall bow, every tongue shall swear.

When the prophet declares that Israel is to be saved, he concludes the sentence with a phrase which at first seems rather out of place, "world without end." However, as we continue through the section, we come to a similar phrase which helps shine a light on this unusual phrase; he declares that all the ends of the earth are to be saved. Sandwiched between these two references to the extremities of the earth is an explanation of the whole purpose of creation--when God made the earth, He did so with an intent that it be inhabited by men who would recognize that He alone is God. Unfortunately, men everywhere have turned to worshipping idols which cannot save. Therefore, He made a decree that men from even the most remote parts of the planet would come to Him in salvation.

This theme is picked up some seven hundred years later as the Apostle Paul penned Romans 10:9-18.

> That if thou shalt confess with thy mouth the Lord Jesus, and shalt

believe in thine heart that God hath raised him from the dead, thou shalt be saved. For with the heart man believeth unto righteousness; and with the mouth confession is made unto salvation. For the scripture saith, Whosoever believeth on him shall not be ashamed. For there is no difference between the Jew and the Greek: for the same Lord over all is rich unto all that call upon him. For whosoever shall call upon the name of the Lord shall be saved. How then shall they call on him in whom they have not believed? and how shall they believe in him of whom they have not heard? and how shall they hear without a preacher? And how shall they preach, except they be sent? as it is written, How beautiful are the feet of them that preach the gospel of peace, and bring glad tidings of good things! But they have not all obeyed the gospel. For Esaias saith, Lord, who hath believed our report? So then faith cometh by hearing, and hearing by the word of God. But I say, Have they not heard? Yes verily, their sound went into all the earth, and their words unto the ends of the world.

    Notice how the New Testament passage repeats the Old Testament's truths about salvation extending to the ends of the earth; moreover, notice that the confession of the mouth is augmented with the belief in the heart in this more refined revelation of the salvation process. When Isaiah declares that every knee will eventually bow and every tongue will eventually confess, his emphasis is on those who will do so in acceptance of His lordship as they inherit eternal salvation. The flip side of this truth is presented in Romans 14:11, when Paul uses this clause to show that some will simply acknowledge His lordship as they are plunged into everlasting damnation.

Let's turn our focus back to the passage which arrested my attention after my excursion into the far-flung corners of our planet. The Revelator goes on to explain that it was the kings of the earth who would bring the glory and honor of their nations into the heavenly city. It wasn't difficult for me to imagine what that procession might be like because I once had a front-row seat as two kings of the earth greeted one another. This once-in-a-lifetime opportunity came at the end of a mission trip to Zimbabwe as I was flying back to Kenya to meet my wife who had been ministering in that eastern African nation while I was speaking in a conference in southern Africa. When I arrived at the airport for my departure, I was greeted with lots of excitement and unusually stringent security. Eventually, I came to learn that the plane I was to fly on had been commandeered by President Robert Mugabe for a flight to Malawi. It was explained to me that it was his custom to fly on the national airline rather than on a private "Air Force One" when he need to travel. The practice was to simply re-route any of the Zimbabwean Air planes which happen to be available at the time. A number of the passengers were simply bumped off the flight and rescheduled and the plane's itinerary was adjusted to accommodate the president's plans. In my case, a stop in Blantyre was added en route to the scheduled destination of Nairobi. In addition, the departure was delayed at least an hour so that the plane would arrive just in time for the scheduled reception by Dr. Bingu wa Mutharika, the Malawian president. When the plane arrived in Malawi, we were greeted by military bands, precision drill teams, dignitaries in formal attire, clerics in their liturgical robes, school children in their most neatly pressed uniforms, and native dancers in their traditional African costumes. I sat and stared out the aircraft's window, watching in close range as all the pageantry, splendor, grandeur, and pomp were displayed as Mr. Mugabe and the First Lady of Zimbabwe exited the plane and were greeted by Dr. wa Mutharika and his wife. It was an experience that can never be forgotten, but it pales in comparison to another quick encounter I had with greatness. It was only a brief few minutes, but those were minutes that will live forever in my memory.

  When Peggy and I were in Calcutta, we stopped by the Missionaries of Charity home with the request to meet Mother Teresa. Honesty, we never expected that we would have the privilege of actually talking with this great woman. To our surprise, the nun who greeted us warmly welcomed us and replied that Mother was busy in a meeting with her staff planning a retreat for the workers. She added that if we would wait just a few minutes she would ask Mother Teresa to see us. Shortly afterwards, the door opened and Mother Teresa entered the room escorted only by the friendly young lady who had greeted us at the door--no fanfare, no bodyguard, none of the trappings that you might expect of a person in her international standing. This saint of God had dropped all that she was doing to visit with strangers who had showed up at her door unannounced and without an appointment or invitation! Her welcome to us was as heartfelt as if we were her closest friends or some outstanding celebrities or officials. But that was Mother Teresa. To her, every human being--royalty or beggar--was of ultimate worth.

She graciously shared with us about her work and about her call to minister to the poor in Calcutta. Then she invited us to visit the home for the dying and the project where the destitute of the streets were being fed. Peggy declined, saying that we had seen the orphanage already but it was her first mission trip to India and that she was already in severe culture shook from what we had seen. Mother patted her hand and replied, "That's okay dear. I understand." The glow in her eyes was a window straight to the heart; it told us that she really did understand--she knew not only the hurts of those on the street, but also the hurt of those of us who are strangers to this level of anguish.

On a later trip to Calcutta, I did have an opportunity to visit the home for the dying where volunteers from around the world were caring for the destitute. Then I made my way to the door where we had been so welcomed before. This time, a simple handwritten note was posted, "Mother is not able to receive guests. She is in prayer." Apparently only God Himself was more important to Mother Teresa than the humans who made a constant trail to her door and into her life.

As we talked with Mother Teresa about all that she had accomplished around the world, we never felt the slightest bit of pride or sense of accomplishment--just an overwhelming gnawing about a job that still was not yet done. But, the outstanding quality of that conversation was the way she turned the discussion away from herself and began to ask us about the mission work that had brought us to India and Sri Lanka. With a light in her eye, she mentioned that she had never been to the areas we would be going to in Sri Lanka. Reading between the lines, we felt that she was excited that someone was going there even if she wasn't.

After a few minutes, she politely mentioned that her staff was waiting for her in a meeting. We asked if we could have a photograph taken with her before she left. When the picture was developed, we both laughed at the way we were stooped just like the aged saint. It was only later that we realized what had actually taken place. Mother Teresa was so gentle and so gracious; yet at the same time, she was such a powerful personality that we bad actually begun to take on her qualities even in just those few minutes. We could only pray that her other qualities of faithful caring and loving will become evident in our lives as well.

Before we left, we asked if we could leave a donation for her work. She called one of her assistants over to receive the check and to see that we were given the proper receipts for the gift. Her parting remarks to us were in reference to Peggy's necklace with a little dove which symbolized the Holy Spirit. "I see that you have the Holy Spirit; I do too," she said.

Micah 6:8 declares, "He hath shewed thee, O man, what is good; and what doth the LORD require of thee, but to do justly, and to love mercy, and to walk humbly with thy God?" Sitting with Mother Teresa, we knew that we were truly in the presence of an individual who had genuinely fulfilled those requirements. Isaiah describes the environment into which God Himself dwells.

> For thus saith the high and lofty One
> that inhabiteth eternity, whose name is
> Holy; I dwell in the high and holy place,
> with him also that is of a contrite and

> humble spirit, to revive the spirit of the humble, and to revive the heart of the contrite ones. (verse 57:15)

For those few minutes, we felt as if we had literally walked into the dwelling place of the Most High! There was no pretension, no fanfare, no grandeur; but we knew that this lady--not the presidents at the African airport--was one of the kings of the earth who would have something worthy of adding to the glory and honor of the New Jerusalem!

Twice in the book of Revelation (verses 1:6, 5:10) and in I Peter (verse 2:9), we are told that believers are kings by divine appointment. Ephesians 2:6 makes it clear that we are already spiritually seated with Christ in heavenly places, and Jesus Himself declared that His followers would literally join Him on thrones to share in His divine rule. (Matthew 19:28) We may not be Mother Teresa, but we will each one have our own bit to contribute to the glory and honor of that city if we stand true through the adversities of this life.

> That the trial of your faith, being much more precious than of gold that perisheth, though it be tried with fire, might be found unto praise and <u>honour</u> and <u>glory</u> at the appearing of Jesus Christ. (I Peter 1:7)
>
> To them who by patient continuance in well doing seek for <u>glory</u> and <u>honour</u> and immortality, eternal life. (Romans 2:7)

John had a revelation concerning the qualities that make for overcoming saints, "And they overcame him by the blood of the Lamb, and by the word of their testimony; and they loved not their lives unto the death." (Revelation 12:11) It is amazing to me that I have heard countless sermons about the power of the blood of the Lamb and innumerable messages on the power of the word of our testimonies. However, the third element in this formula seems to be a point which is seldom mentioned--we must come to the place that we are so determined to stand for God that we are ready and willing to give our lives for the cause.

The Revelator continues in his description of those who will bring glory and honor into the heavenly city by saying that nothing which defiles can enter in. In the Old Testament, we find that defilement was associated with certain foods, certain sexual practices, and touching dead bodies; however, the New Testament makes it clear that defilement has to do with what comes out of the mouth and the spirit of a man.

> But those things which proceed out of the mouth come forth from the heart; and they defile the man. (Matthew 15:18)
>
> There is nothing from without a man, that entering into him can defile him: but the things which come out of him, those are they that defile the man...And he saith unto them, Are ye so without understanding also? Do ye not perceive, that whatsoever thing from without entereth into the man, it cannot defile him…All these evil things come from within, and defile the man. (Mark 7:15, 18, 23)
>
> And the tongue is a fire, a world of iniquity: so is the tongue among our members, that it defileth the whole body, and setteth on fire the course of nature; and it is set on fire of hell.

(James 3:6)

To be able to enter the New Jerusalem and to bring glory into it, we must have our hearts and tongues totally purified and radically sanctified. John adds that those who work abomination will also be barred from that celestial city. Although we may immediately think of the sexual perverts parading down the streets on Gay Pride Day, a simple look at the scripture will bring this truth a lot closer to home. According to Proverbs 6:16-19, there are six things that God hates and seven areas which He considers abominations:

    1) a proud look,
    2) a lying tongue,
    3) hands that shed innocent blood,
    4) a heart that devises wicked imaginations,
    5) feet that run to mischief,
    6) a false witness that speaks lies, and
    7) one who sows discord among the brethern.

Though only a few of us knew anything about it, one of my college students had been converted from a homosexual lifestyle. When some clues about his past began to leak out and were circulated among the other students, one of the supposedly spiritual members of the class came to me quoting a passage which branded the young man as an abomination. I listened patiently to the exhortation and then asked the student to read the passage I have just cited. My point was that the murmuring was as much an abomination as his homosexuality. Then I pointed out that he had been delivered out of that lifestyle while the present student body was still actively participating in the abomination of sowing discord. To qualify to bring glory and honor into the kingdom of God, we must move beyond our own human righteousness, which the prophet Isaiah labeled as filthy rags (verse 64:6) into a divinely generated righteousness.

    The unfortunate thing is that we too often feel that we can substitute our own accomplishments for the godly purity which only Christ can impart. Think about the Old Testament account of the golden shields in Solomon's temple. After they were stolen by the Egyptian king, Rehoboam made brass shields to replace them. (II Chronicles 12:10) Certainly, there was no one who was fooled by the inferior substitutes, but we Christians try an even more preposterous substitution trick when we try to fashion our Christian lives with wood, hay, and stubble rather than authentic gold, silver, and precious stones. (I Corinthians 12:10) The admonition of Jesus Christ to the self-righteous Laodicean church was that they need to come to Him to buy gold which had been tried and proven rather than to rely upon their presumed resources. (Revelation 3:18)

    The marble of the Taj Mahal, no matter how gorgeous it might be, could not add any grandeur to the precious stones which make up the walls and foundations or the transparent gold of the New Jerusalem. In like manner, we must realize that none of our human accomplishments can add to the glory and honor of that city; in actuality, we would only distract from it. However, the Lord is calling each of us to become the glory and honor of our nation so that we will have something to contribute to the splendor of the city. As the time draws near for the great parade of nations to enter into the New Jerusalem and present their tribute to God, we must present ourselves as righteous saints with robes washed white and spotless in the blood of the Lamb. We must all come to the same realization that Paul had in Romans chapter seven that in ourselves there in nothing worthwhile.

The only solution is to affirm as Paul did in Galatians 2:20 that our own lives have been crucified with Christ and that the lives we are able to live are only because of Christ living inside of us and that our very existence is simply through faith in the Son of God who loves us and gave Himself for us. Because it is Christ in us which is the hope of glory (Colossians 1:27), there is something in us which can indeed bring glory and honor into the heavenly city.

There is one last point we need to consider as we ponder how we are to bring glory and honor into the heavenly kingdom: we must gather more of the jewels of each nation by bringing the gospel to every kindred, tongue, people, and nation. Then they, too, can join us as the glory and honor of their nations to be presented at the foot of God's throne.

Going into all the world to present the message of salvation is not only our privilege; it is also our mandate. (Mark 16:15-16) It is a personal mandate to share the message individually (preach the gospel to every creature); yet, it is a global imperative (go ye into all the world). Our mandate is one of not only evangelism, but also of spiritual development in the form of solid teaching and instruction. (Matthew 28:18-20) To fulfill this mandate, we must--as Mother Teresa pointed out--have the supernatural enablement of the Holy Spirit. (Luke 24:46-49) At that point, our effectiveness will be through who and what we are, not what we do. We shall be witnesses, not just people who do witnessing! (Acts 1:8) Again, we see that our only hope of being able to bring glory and honor into the eternal city is through the power and character of the Godhead dwelling inside of us!